As catechists, it i
context of the lif‹
of the church: ev‹
the popes from P‹

, ————— ———— ——— ——— ——— gives cate-
chists the gift of reading and reflecting on church documents, a largely
untapped resource for envisioning a sense of church and church mission for today's context. The excerpts that Daniella has chosen give us
a peek into the richness of these documents and remind all catechists
of the important work that we do, guided by the Spirit. With evocative
questions at the end of each chapter, this is an excellent resource for
either individual or group reflection.

〰 **JANE E. REGAN**, *Associate Professor of Religious Education, Boston College*
School of Theology and Ministry; Director, Continuing Education at STM

Conversion is always effective communication! In *Evangelization and
Catechesis*, Daniella Zsupan-Jerome has brilliantly approached today's
pertinent evangelization topics from various perspectives—historical,
theological, spiritual, and pastoral. It is a "must read" for those
desiring a vibrant, life-transforming faith and for those who wish to
animate others with the gospel of Jesus Christ in our digital culture.

〰 **VERY REV. DAVID G. CARON, OP, D.MIN.**,
Vicar of Evangelization, Archdiocese of New Orleans

As always, Daniella Zsupan-Jerome does not want to "tell" us the right
things to think or read or do. She invites us into conversation and is
ready to learn alongside us. What a gift to have these church documents lifted up to us as the treasures they are and then be invited to
unpack them together. Daniella does not just write about evangelization and catechesis—she models it beautifully! Mixed in with these
nuggets from Tradition and Scripture are down-to-earth, relatable
stories and questions for reflection that seek to move us forward in
ministry emboldened to proclaim the Good News in our own times.

〰 **ANNE JAMIESON, D.MIN.**, *Director of Catechesis,*
Diocese of Hamilton, Ontario

Those dedicated to evangelization and catechesis will find in Dr. Daniella Zsupan-Jerome's newest book not only a concise theological summary of contemporary church teaching on the topic but also a spiritual guide to refresh one on the mission. Highlighting the heart of the matter, she inspires those of us in the field to encourage new life in others through our own brokenness.

↬ **DR. JOHN OSMAN**, *Director of Evangelization and Catechesis, St. Vincent de Paul Parish, Austin, Texas*

Daniella Zsupan-Jerome has written an introduction to the documents of the church that is a form of *lectio divina*. She does not treat these documents as proof texts. The documents become through her prose an occasion to contemplate the gift of divine love revealed in Jesus Christ and mediated in the life of the church.

↬ **TIMOTHY O'MALLEY**, *Director for the Notre Dame Center for Liturgy*

Daniella Zsupan-Jerome has created an informative and prayerful resource for those engaged in catechesis. Daniella's approach distinguishes itself by its integration of essential, life-giving principles with today's real experience of communicating the faith in love, achieving a fruitful harmony between the two. Very helpful for catechist formation or as a gift to generous catechists!

↬ **DR. JAMES PAULEY**, *Associate Professor of Theology and Catechetics, Franciscan University of Steubenville*

EVANGELIZATION AND CATECHESIS

The ESSENTIAL CATECHIST'S BOOKSHELF

Evangelization *and* Catechesis

Echoing *the* Good News
through the Documents
of the Church

Daniella Zsupan-Jerome, Ph.D.

TWENTY-THIRD
PUBLICATIONS
twentythirdpublications.com

Dedication

To Mary, Mother of the Word

Teach us to listen, to say yes, and to hold mystery in our hearts.

Pray for us as we echo the Good News of your Son.

In truth and in love.

TWENTY-THIRD PUBLICATIONS
1 Montauk Avenue, Suite 200, New London, CT 06320
(860) 437-3012 » (800) 321-0411 » www.twentythirdpublications.com

COVER PHOTO: ALAIN PINOGES/CIRIC

ISBN: 978-1-62785-249-4
Library of Congress Catalog Card Number: 2016956546
Printed in the U.S.A.

Contents

Invitation to Inspiration *1*

1 What is Evangelization? *3*

2 How to Begin *15*

3 Must Love People: A Ministry
  Animated by Love. *26*

4 Centered on Christ: Our Primary
  and Essential Mystery *36*

5 The Life-Giving Spirit of Catechesis *46*

6 Catechesis as a Moment
  of Evangelization *57*

7 Communicating the Word of God *71*

8 Catechesis and the Way of Beauty *86*

Epilogue: Ave *95*

INVITATION TO INSPIRATION

Evangelization. This is a word every catechist has come across, whether at a pastoral staff meeting, at a ministry conference, in the language of diocesan statements and communiqués, or in one of the myriad blogs, videos, webinars, podcasts, lists, and articles that populate the typical Catholic ministry social media newsfeed. It is a word that is part of today's Catholic professional ministerial vocabulary.

Evangelization is important, we know. The term comes up as a reminder of a greater purpose, a greater context of the work of catechesis. It is like an invisible thread that pulls catechesis toward the heart of the church, toward the central meaning of what the church is and what we as her members are called to be. It is a term without which catechesis does not make sense—it gives the catechetical task its greater purpose and context.

Of late, the term has gained a qualifier: the *new* evangelization. What is new about the new evangelization has sparked pastoral discussions and generated articles and presentation topics with gusto, and it shows us that evangelization is not only an important word but also a dynamic one. Understanding what it means and what it calls us to in catechesis is an ongoing conversation.

This book holds an invitation for catechists to enter into this ongoing conversation. Understanding evangelization (whether old or "the new") is not just an academic exercise. It is rather an act of taking a step back from the work of catechesis to behold the bigger picture. Especially on our busiest days of ministerial overload, this big-picture image can be inspiring and remind us why it is we do what we do.

The hope of this book, then, is to offer the big-picture view of catechesis, and to do it in an inspiring, energizing way. Ever since my days in graduate school, I have found true inspiration in the church's rich array of documents: from encyclicals to homilies, I have found these to be acutely aware, balanced, pastorally sensitive, and above all, inspiring. Church documents may be the Catholic tradition's best-kept secret—a best-kept secret because few outside of academia may sit and reflect readily with them. One hope of this book is to widen the audience of these amazing resources.

In discussing evangelization and catechesis, this book lays out a path where each of the stepping stones comes from a church document. Each of the chapters of this book is built around a selected passage from a papal document, ranging from the work of Pope Paul VI to Pope Francis, and spanning the past four decades. In each chapter we pause with a passage in order to be inspired and to gain another glimpse at the bigger picture.

Daniella Zsupan-Jerome

What is Evangelization? The Big Picture *of* *the* Big Picture

Such an exhortation seems to us to be of capital importance, for the presentation of the Gospel message is not an optional contribution for the Church. It is the duty incumbent on her by the command of the Lord Jesus, so that people can believe and be saved. This message is indeed necessary. It is unique. It cannot be replaced. It does not permit either indifference, syncretism or accommodation. It is a question of people's salvation. It is the beauty of the Revelation that it represents. It brings with it a wisdom that is not of this world. It is able to stir up by itself faith—faith that rests on the power of God. (Cf. 1 Corinthians 2:5) It is truth. It merits having the apostle consecrate to it all his time and all his energies, and to sacrifice for it, if necessary, his own life.

FROM PARAGRAPH 5, *ON EVANGELIZATION IN THE MODERN WORLD*
POPE PAUL VI, DECEMBER 8, 1975

What an inspiring, beautiful passage! Through these words shines true conviction: a stability of heart rooted in the truth of the gospel, and a certainty of faith that clears away our foggy ambiguities and invites us to rest in truth. One of my favorite keepsake items is a small clay sculpture of a palm of a hand, extended flat as a bird nestles in its very middle. It brings to mind for me the psalmist's words: "Return, my soul to your rest; the LORD has been very good to you" (Psalm 116:7). This passage evokes for me the same sense of stability, rest, and certainty in the grace of God that holds and preserves each of us.

To be sure, the above passage does not call us to passive rest or to a lazy lounging in the hammock of God's providence. It is a rousing passage, one that is meant to enkindle in us the passion to serve, to help reveal glimmers of God's reign. How then it is restful? It is restful not in its lack of activity, but rather in the sense of rootedness and stability it provides. The restless soul comes to rest in God's palm, all the while animating us to holy action: to serve in a way that is of God and for God. We are no longer in charge—and this thought is restful relief in itself, especially in the busy ministry of catechesis. Through this passage the Spirit blows with a mighty wind to send away all obscurity and haze, numbing ambiguity and sense of being overwhelmed that hangs on us like fog. This is truth and we rest in its clarity.

This passage comes from Pope Paul VI's 1975 apostolic exhortation *Evangelii Nuntiandi* (*On Evangelization in the Modern World*). This was a document created just ten years after the Second Vatican Council, and it reflected on this ten-year anniversary quite intentionally. Building on the work of the 1974 synod of bishops, which treated the topic of evangelization, Pope Paul VI reflected on how the church is engaging the world with the gospel message, and how the church can be more reflective, intentional, and systematic about this. In the post-Vatican II era this document has become a fundamental starting point for thinking about evangelization.

On Evangelization in the Modern World tells us at length about evangelization, the greater umbrella under which catechesis finds itself. We can ponder in this document evangelization's definition, content, method, beneficiaries, workers, and spirit. In the context of this greater presentation, this passage here focuses in on something essential; it points out that the presentation of the gospel message is an essential act for the church. So essential is it, in fact, that it is not merely something that the church *does*; at the very heart of the matter, the presentation of the gospel message is what the church *is*. As the document tells us elsewhere: the church exists in order to evangelize (EN 14). Evangelization is the church's deepest identity. Evangelization as *the deepest identity* of the church may present for us a new way of thinking. Often when we think about the church, a typical image that comes to mind is about the institution: in some beautiful hall at the Vatican, bishops, cardinals, and monsignors gathered to meet with the pope. Or, the church may bring to mind Sunday worship, focused on the liturgical celebration of the assembly as led by the presider. For most Catholics, this latter image focuses in even further on the Eucharist, the real presence of the Lord in our midst in sacramental form. For catechists, directors of religious education, and other ministers of the word in pastoral work, the church may also evoke rules and regulations, communiqués from the diocesan office, proper protocol, liturgical norms, and canon law. The church is also known for the good that it does in education, health care, service organizations, and promoting or supporting causes of social justice. Of course, this list is incomplete. But imagining church in all of these cases is associated with certain people, certain places, certain activities, or certain norms and values. These certain elements are all good and true. But is there a bigger picture, one that brings together all of these mental pictures into one cohesive whole?

The answer is evangelization. As the deepest identity of the church, evangelization reminds us that all of the church's various manifestations exist for one thing and one thing only: to present the gospel of salvation of Jesus Christ so that people can believe and be saved. The pope exists in his specific role for this. The bishop exists in his role for this. Our sacramental celebrations exist for this. Our works of charity and justice exist for this. Our teachings, rules, norms, laws, and directives exist for this. Our catechetical ministry exists for this. This is the mission statement that holds it all together, and it is a mission statement in the most profound sense of the term, embracing the risen Lord's own parting words to the apostles: "Go into the whole world and proclaim the gospel to every creature" (Mark 16:15). Since those days of the apostles receiving this Great Commission, the church exists to evangelize, and to carry out this mission in all of our roles, teaching, and activities.

GOSPEL

Proclaiming the gospel is at the center of the task of evangelization. But what is the gospel? We hear this word at every Mass, and we know by our rituals that it is special. When the gospel is read, we stand to honor it as it is proclaimed. We sign our head, lips, and heart along with the presider in preparation for receiving it. Having heard it, we offer praise directly to Jesus Christ.

The word "gospel" may also bring special images or objects to mind. Most likely, we think of the Bible, or perhaps a beautifully ornate lectionary or book of the gospels used at Mass. Our family Bibles, cherished and displayed in many of our homes, may also come to mind. We may think of Matthew, Mark, Luke, and John, the four evangelists, and may even be familiar with their symbols in Christian art: the man, the lion, the ox, and the eagle. Like evangelization, the gospel is part of our Catholic vocabulary and symbol system. While it is a commonly used word, it has uncommon meaning, and it is meaning we may not be entirely sure about. What are we really proclaiming when we are proclaiming the gospel?

Etymology is helpful here. We inherit the word "gospel" from the Old English *godspel*, which means "good story," and it refers back to the Greek word *euangelion*, which is also the source of our word evangelization. The Greek root *euangelion* means "glad tidings" or "good news," and evangelization, then, is the bringing forth of the good news, the sharing of glad tidings. Along these lines, the proclamation of the gospel is the announcing of that which is profoundly good news. If evangelization is the church's deepest identity, then, as catechists, we are called to be good news in our very being and to offer good news as a witness to the world. Given this fundamental place of the good news, Pope Francis has a point when he tells us that "an evangelizer must never look like someone who has just come back from a funeral" (*The Joy of the Gospel [Evangelii Gaudium]*, 10).

The "good news" is such a simple phrase that we must be careful that its meaning does not become banal, especially when applied to evangelization. After all, a diagnosis of no cavities at the dentist is good news. A gallon of gas under $2, the cancellation of a tedious meeting, a tax refund: these are all serendipitous pleasures of our daily lives that we would call moments of good news. Is this what we are called to embrace as an evangelizing church? What about the reality of all the other meaningless, painful, frustrating, or burdensome moments of our day? Keeping in mind that one of our central symbols is the crucifix, we must continue to search for a deeper, more complex meaning of the "good news" than those little daily moments when things go our way.

Our passage from *Evangelii Nuntiandi* at the beginning of this chapter offers us some clues. It tells us that the gospel is *"necessary, unique, cannot be replaced, does not permit either indifference, syncretism or accommodation, and it is a question of people's salvation."* Nothing can replace or dilute the good news of the gospel. This good news is no longer in the category of $2 gas or no cavities. We are invited into a much deeper reality, which is not just a good bit of news, but Good News itself. This Good News is both fundamental and transcendent, or, as *Evangelii Nuntiandi* tells us above, *"it brings with it a wisdom that is not of this world."*

There is good news and there is the Good News. As church, we are called to present the latter and to do it precisely in the context of life's meaningless, painful, frustrating, and burdensome circumstances. The Good News is the Word yearning to be uttered exactly in the mess of all this, and to bring therein joy, hope, transformation, healing, and new life. One powerful illustration of this appears in the words of the angel who visits the shepherds on the night of Jesus' birth. As the Gospel of Luke narrates for us:

> Now there were shepherds in that region living in the fields and keeping the night watch over their flock. The angel of the Lord appeared to them and the glory of the Lord shone around them and they were struck with great fear. The angel said to them, "Do not be afraid; for behold I proclaim to you good news of great joy that will be for all the people. For today in the city of David a savior has been born for you who is Messiah and Lord. And this will be a sign for you: you will find an infant wrapped in swaddling clothes lying in a manger."

And suddenly there was a multitude of the heavenly host with the angel, praising God and saying:
"Glory to God in the highest and on earth peace
to those on whom his favor rests." (LUKE 2:8–14)

Scripture scholars remind us that the shepherds of Jesus' time
were the epitome of "messy." They lived with the flock, in nature, and therefore literally on the margins of civilized society.
Because they were outdoors people who worked with animals,
we can imagine them as messy in the most concrete sense,
with some dirt around their fingernails, stray wool on their
clothes, and mud on their feet. The angel's announcement to
the shepherds brings the Good News into these earthy, messy
circumstances. Given the no-frills setting, the angel makes
present the Good News in no uncertain terms: it is Good
News of great joy, for everyone. It is news about a savior born
for all, a savior who is the fulfillment of hopes and promises of
long ago, hopes and promises that are ingrained in the Jewish
imagination. This savior is an answer to their long-inherited
yearnings. This great news is undeniable—it bursts forth with
a whole choir of angels singing the *Gloria* to punctuate the
announcement.

Imagining the lives of shepherds, we wonder about the
hunger and yearning they may have felt for the Good News.
The angel makes it clear that the Good News is not just about
avoiding the wolf who may menace the flock, or about finding
good pasture for the sheep, or about a good price for wool at
the market. It is Good News for all the people, and it fulfills
the yearning at their *very identity* as the people of Israel. It is
Good News that speaks to the Jewish identity, so much so
that for the Christian church, the sharing of this Good News
becomes Christian identity. Evangelization is the church's
deepest identity (EN 14).

The Good News for the people of Israel that the angel is talking about is, of course, the birth of Jesus Christ, who is Savior and Messiah. Savior and Messiah are two titles that reveal for us that the cause for our joy is not just about his birth, but also about all that he will accomplish in his life, death, and resurrection. The Good News of Jesus Christ embraces all of this: the fact of his incarnation, the reality of his passion, the truth of his resurrection, the joy of his ascension. This is Good News revealed to us beautifully in the example of his life, a life that gave life to us all. Christ's life, death, and resurrection reveal Good News in profound ways:

- His incarnation as God-with-Us reveals to us the intimate love of God, and God's immense desire for relationship with us. We are not abandoned in our mess and misery. Instead, God pours out his love in Jesus Christ to join our reality and to walk with us so that we can walk with God.

- His life and ministry reveal to us glimpses of the kingdom of God, a reality in which God's peace, justice, and mercy triumph and all creation exists in right relationship with God.

- His passion reveals to us God's self-gift: from the Last Supper to the cross, we are faced with the self-giving love of God in a way that knows no bounds.

- His resurrection reveals to us our hope. Death no longer has the final word, as the risen Lord shatters its bonds and offers us eternal life.

- His ascension reveals to us the invitation and the path to our joy in our eternal communion with God.

The Good News is the summation of these points, a phrase that expresses a total transformation of our horizons, infinitely expanding our hope and possibility in light of Christ the Savior. This sense of total hope and possibility is perhaps most tangible to us in the Easter season of the liturgical year. It is the glow of taper candles filling the darkened church; it is the sense of celebration witnessing the rites of initiation; it is the triumphant Alleluias ringing out from the choir; it is the "I do" we say to affirm our own baptismal vows with the hope to do better to honor these; it is the sprinkle of water felt on the skin; it is the worship space full of fragrant lilies after weeks of Lenten simplicity. Anything is possible in the light of Easter morning.

Of course, our whole liturgical year in all of its feasts and seasons invites us into the reality of the Good News. But it is also true that the church is born of the Easter Sunday experience, and it is during Easter that our liturgy presents us with gestures, images, symbols, and stories that reveal the heart of who we are as people of Good News. The words "Christ is risen—risen indeed" resound in the Christian heart at all times.

CATECHESIS CONNECTION

Pope Paul VI tells us about the importance of the proclamation of the gospel message as essential to evangelization, so much so that it is the very identity of the church. How does this touch the work of catechesis? Consider the following scene.

On a given Sunday morning at church, the liturgy is unfolding as usual. First reading, psalm, second reading, gospel, homily. After the homily, a select group seated in the reserved pews up front begins to stir. They are the RCIA group: catechumens, catechists, and sponsors. After having heard the word proclaimed, they are about to line up to receive the lectionary and then process out to reflect as a group on what they have heard. A brief musical interlude accompanies their dismissal.

In this scene, it is clear that the proclamation of the gospel message occurs at a moment distinct from the catechesis. We hear the gospel proclaimed from the pulpit as one of the readings of Mass, and catechesis picks up where this proclamation leaves off. If catechesis is distinct from this more direct proclamation of the gospel from the pulpit, does catechesis engage at all in the proclamation of the gospel as evangelization?

The answer is yes. If evangelization is the very identity of the church, then the proclamation of the gospel message must take place in some form through *everything* that the church does. This everything includes clear and direct examples, such as the actual proclamation of the gospel during Sunday liturgy, but it also includes a myriad of more complex, subtle, or implied ways. In short, in a different way, the proclamation of the gospel continues for the RCIA even after they are dismissed for their discussion.

Proclamation of the gospel is broader than formal communication done from the pulpit. It is the sharing of the Good News made manifest in Christ's life, death, and resurrection, and done in a way that addresses us here and today. Even though, in our RCIA scenario, the gospel has been formally proclaimed, the work of catechesis after the dismissal has ample room to allow for this Good News to continue to echo in conversation and reflection. Just as the angel brought the Good News directly to the shepherds, the Good News is not a stand-apart abstraction, but rather a relational movement that addresses the hearer directly. Catechesis works at helping to clarify this address to each hearer and to help explore how each mind and heart may respond to the address of the Word in faith. Throughout it all, the Good News continues to echo.

Catechesis, in the Greek origins of the word, means just this: to echo or resound. What it is echoing or resounding is the Good News, whether through instruction, discussion, reflection, prayer, rites, and rituals that mark it as a process, or, as we will see in the next chapter, even the manner and tone of interactions that take place between the people involved. All of this finds its source and purpose in the greater evangelizing identity of the church.

✹ *Questions for Contemplation*

- What is the Good News? How would you describe the Good News of Jesus Christ in your own words?

- Pray and reflect on Luke 2:8–14. Imagine yourself in the field with the shepherds as the angel comes to announce the Good News of Jesus Christ. How does this passage speak to you?

- In what ways do you see evangelization expressed as the deepest identity of the church? What are some different examples of the church being Good News?

- In your own catechetical ministry, how do see the echoing of the Good News as central to what you do?

✹ *Prayer*

Almighty Father, you reach out to us in love
    through your Son Jesus Christ,
who came to bring us the Good News of salvation
    for all your people.
Bless our work in the ministry of catechesis
so that all that we do may be both rooted in and directed
    toward the sharing of your Son's Good News.

May this Good News reach especially those
   who are yearning for its promise
in the struggles, challenges, and uncertainties of life.
We ask this through your Son, who is our Savior
   and Messiah,
by the life-giving power of the Holy Spirit.
Amen.

How to Begin: Called *to a* Witness *of* Life

For the Church, the first means of evangelization is the witness of an authentically Christian life, given over to God in a communion that nothing should destroy and at the same time given over to one's neighbor with limitless zeal. As we said recently to a group of lay people, "Modern man listens more willingly to witnesses than to teachers, and if he does listen to teachers, it is because they are witnesses." Saint Peter expressed this well when he held up the example of a reverent and chaste life that wins over even without a word those who refuse to obey the word. (Cf. 1 Peter 3:1.) It is therefore primarily by her conduct and by her life that the Church will evangelize the world, in other words by her living witness of fidelity to the Lord Jesus—the witness of poverty and detachment, of freedom in the face of the powers of this world, in short, the witness of sanctity.

PARAGRAPH 41, *ON EVANGELIZATION IN THE MODERN WORLD*
POPE PAUL VI, DECEMBER 8, 1975

Recall some of your first moments in your ministry as a cat-echist. Perhaps it was early summer, and you were staring at a pile of paperwork for Vacation Bible School, applications and forms submitted by parents on behalf of their little ones. Or it was late summer, and you were anxiously planning your five-minute announcement to address the assembly from the pulpit next Sunday about the RCIA. Or it was the first time you were handed the lectionary in front of a sizable group of four- to eight-year-olds as you prepared to process out with them for Children's Liturgy of the Word. Or you were tasked to plan the confirmation program for the parish's teens, as pan-icked words echoed in your mind: *the bishop will be here for this.*

In each of these examples, the magnitude of the task was evident. What may not have been evident right away was how to begin. You had curriculum books and activity binders to provide a map for the task ahead, but in a moment of stillness you may have sat with and prayed about a deeper question: *Lord, how am I going to do this?*

The selected passage above from *On Evangelization in the Modern World* talks about the fundamental "how" of evangeli-zation. It does not mention curriculum books, activity bind-ers, programs, steps, or processes; and perhaps that is for the better. While these resources are good and useful, sometimes the desire for knowing *how* transcends the selection of a par-ticular textbook or activity. Sometimes the desire for knowing how is a desire for reencountering a passion for the work and for the ultimate answer to why this ministry is worthwhile and meaningful. Knowing how in the deepest sense is recall-ing what has led us to this point, to serving in the ministry of catechesis.

Along these lines, the passage above offers inspiration for the still moment when we pray the question "Lord, how am I going to do this?" in the broadest sense possible. In response to the how, it offers us a disposition, or a way of being: being a witness. As the above passage tells us, this is the most true and compelling method of evangelization.

TEACHING BY CONDUCT AND BY LIFE

Gabriel Moran, an important scholar of Catholic religious education, reflected on the activity of teaching in his 1997 book *Showing How*. According to Moran, teaching has a much broader meaning than classroom instruction, where an expert is explaining matters to a group of listeners. A better definition of teaching for Moran, especially when it comes to religious education, is "showing how to live." In the above passage from *On Evangelization in the Modern World*, we see the same principle applied to the church and the church's evangelizing mission. Evangelization is not simply classroom-type instruction about matters of faith. Instead, it is the church showing how to live, and to live as Jesus promised us: to the fullest (John 10:10), and unto eternal life (John 4:14).

To be sure, classroom-type instruction on all levels is indispensable for this, and much of it takes place in the context of catechesis. But classroom-type instruction, even in catechesis, is but one important way of showing how. *On Evangelization in the Modern World* reminds us that there is a more fundamental approach to sharing the Good News, and to showing how to live: "*It is therefore primarily by her conduct and by her life that the Church will evangelize the world.*" As we ponder and pray over the question of "how," our starting point is to reflect our own conduct and way of life, especially as members of the church in the context of working with people in ministry.

As you think about your own religious education experience, recall the best, most impactful teacher you have ever had. Perhaps the person who comes to mind was a family member, a catechist, youth minister, peer, pastor, high-school teacher or college professor. Whoever this person was, they likely stand out in your mind because of a clear and discernible connection between the content of faith they taught you and the example they set. (Perhaps the example they set *was* the content of faith in some cases!) They did not just inform you about the faith; they showed you how to live it by living it themselves. They modeled passion for, and deep commitment to, the faith in a way that impressed you. In the resonance between who they were and what they handed on, they revealed the faith by their whole manner of being. In the language of *On Evangelization in the Modern World*, they were a witness.

In *On Evangelization in the Modern World*, Pope Paul VI tells us: *"Modern man listens more willingly to witnesses than to teachers, and if he does listen to teachers, it is because they are witnesses."* Is it still possible to listen to and indeed learn from a great and scholarly teacher who shares with us deep insight into a discipline? Of course it is; listening to a great lecture is very edifying. But the witness has the advantage in that people listen more willingly. Along with content, the witness also offers of himself or herself, or as we say in common parlance, the witness "speaks from the heart." The witness shares with conviction because "showing how to live" means first knowing that which has been life-giving and transformative for oneself. It is difficult to resist listening to such an authentic story.

That the witness offers of himself or herself is an important point to pause with. To offer oneself, or to give the gift of oneself, is an inspiring concept in Catholic theology, one that is layered with beautiful meaning. We find examples of self-gift all throughout the life, death, resurrection, and ascension of Jesus Christ:

- We can see the incarnation as God the Father's self-gift to humankind in the birth of his Son.

- We can see God's self-gift in the myriad ways Christ ministered to the people of his time: healing, reconciling, forgiving, and freeing wherever he went.

- We see self-gift in the institution of the Eucharist, in which Christ offers us bread and wine as his Body and Blood in the context of the Last Supper. We see self-gift in the act of foot-washing in the Gospel of John.

- We see self-gift in the sacrifice of his life on the cross, and in all that leads up to it during his passion.

- We see self-gift in the resurrection and the ascension, and in the invitation these contain to live eternally in Christ.

- We see self-gift in the sending of the Holy Spirit, the Advocate, who continues to breathe life into the body of Christ as the church.

God gifting Godself to humankind in these and other ways is a consistent element of how God has related with us in salvation history. Because we are members of the church and called to be witnesses, this dynamic of self-gift is important to reflect on and attend to in the way we engage in ministry.

In our everyday language, the word witness is both a noun and a verb. To be a witness is to have firsthand experience of an event in such a way that it becomes evidence and gives the person indisputable credibility when he or she offers testimony about this. To witness means to have such a firsthand experience, or to testify and provide evidence thereof.

In the language of the church, the word "witness" is also closely connected with "martyr"; in fact, the Greek word for witness that we find in the New Testament is *martys*. The close association between witness and martyrdom recalls the importance of self-gift. It also reminds us that our martyrs, whether those in the early days of the church or those who suffer this fate today, are people giving evidence of their firsthand experience of Jesus Christ. Very often, a martyr is thought of as a victim or a sacrifice, and indeed they do suffer these realities. But fundamentally, they merit the title because their example gives evidence of their deep conviction and faith.

WITNESS OF SANCTITY

Are we called to martyrdom? *On Evangelization in the Modern World* guides us in this direction as it calls us to a "witness of sanctity," which it describes as a *"living witness of fidelity to the Lord Jesus—the witness of poverty and detachment, of freedom in the face of the powers of this world."* A witness is a person unequivocally committed to Christ, and this commitment becomes evident in the way he or she lives. Poverty, detachment, and freedom are three ways to describe this unequivocal commitment. We must be careful to avoid reading into these a political leaning or commentary. Poverty, detachment, and freedom speak about an undivided heart, and clarity about who we are and whose we are.

Poverty is a disposition of openness; it is our empty open hands held up to God. A witness of poverty recognizes that it is God who gives us life and sustains us with grace, and that none of our efforts or machinations can replace this. No matter how much we amass, whether it is money, food, property, fine things, or friends on Facebook, none of these fulfills our deepest desires. A witness of poverty thus leaves room for God's grace as the only gift that ultimately satisfies.

Detachment follows from poverty's openness to God. Detachment is poverty's end: it is openness not just in the present moment but also directed toward our ultimate home in God. As the parable of the rich fool in Luke's gospel tells us, it is futile to amass worldly goods in bigger and bigger barns (Luke 12:16–21). On the night that our life is demanded of us, these will amount to nothing. Unlike the ancient Egyptians who built tombs filled with goods for the afterlife, the Christian leaves this life as simply as he or she entered it. In eternal life our existence is not purely spiritual: we believe in the resurrection of our bodies and hope for an eternity that includes the body. But when it comes to other temporal things, we know they pass away; as Isaiah tells us, "the earth [will] wear out like a garment and its inhabitants die like flies" (Isaiah 51:6). A witness of detachment is awareness of our finitude, all the while living life with the hope of eternity. It is a life set on storing up treasure in heaven.

Freedom is a cherished word for us—it is a concept constitutive of American identity. Since the colonial beginnings of the United States, people have sought out this land to find freedom and opportunity. A witness of freedom also echoes some of this idea of new hope and possibility. But the quoted passage above also tells us that this freedom is particular in that it is *"in the face of the powers of this world."* Freedom in this sense is a disposition that follows from detachment. It is detachment not only from material things but also from being beholden to the powers of our world. What are these powers? Values, mindsets, ideologies, and broadly held assumptions that generate worldviews. These worldviews may certainly have elements of goodness, truth, and even beauty to them. But they become problematic when they overshadow or replace the gospel as our worldview par excellence. Freedom in the face of the powers of this world is freedom to remain beholden to the gospel as one's ultimate way of making sense of life. In this, a witness to freedom is a witness to possibility and to hope—key elements of the gospel message.

The dispositions of poverty, detachment, and freedom build on each other and together give the shape of a witness of sanctity. Sanctity is a beautiful word, and one that immediately brings to mind sacred spaces and objects, or perhaps remarkable people whose faces we now meet on holy picture cards. In this light, a call to a witness of sanctity all of a sudden seems like a sky-high standard. How can we possibly witness like St. John Paul II or St. Teresa of Kolkata?

John Climacus, a seventh-century monk, also thought about our path toward the witness of sanctity. His reflection resulted in a now-famous image: a ladder connecting heaven and earth, showing people climbing upward. Called his "Ladder of Divine Ascent," the image was later painted as an icon and has inspired the prayerful reflection of generations since. The Ladder of Divine Ascent is a complex image. The ladder shows a procession of figures climbing steadily upward; their goal at the top is Christ himself, who awaits them with open arms. Angels look on encouragingly from above, but they are not the only audience to the climb. A bevy of demons buzz around the lower parts of the ladder, poking at and targeting the climbers. They succeed in making a number of figures tumble and fall downward to their realm.

This is a sobering image, to be sure. We can rightly wonder if the dispositions of poverty, detachment, and freedom might make us lighter on this climb, lessen our burdens, and help to move us upward and away from the distractions and temptations that would lead to our downfall.

Sanctity is not about a perfectly lived life. It is about a life lived climbing the Ladder of Divine Ascent with our eyes focused on the open arms of Christ waiting at the top. Our open hands held up to him to receive grace all through our life find their final fulfillment in these open arms. A witness of sanctity is living this climb. It is walking light enough that we can make our way upward. It is having clarity and focus on our goal and taking each step in life so that it leads us toward it. It is making sure that temptations, distractions, and even sin do not lead to a downward plunge. It is knowing where to place our hands and feet so that we are supported along the way. If teaching is showing how to live, it is also showing how to make this climb. A witness of sanctity in teaching is revealing the ladder, showing where to step, and guiding along to where it leads.

CATECHESIS CONNECTION

The selected passage for this chapter from *On Evangelization in the Modern World* teaches us that the how of evangelization is a comprehensive witness of life, which ultimately is a witness of sanctity, or a witness of the certainty of our belonging to God. Religious education in this context becomes much more than just content delivery—as religious educators we are called to show how to live.

Given this broader understanding of both evangelization and religious education, the role of catechetical instruction becomes important to define. In your experience as a catechist, it is likely that much of your time is spent in planning for or carrying out actual instruction: lessons and activities around given topics. How can this become part of showing how to live? How can the catechist become a witness in his and her ministry? How do we infuse instruction with a witness of sanctity?

Understanding teaching as showing how to live is nowhere more important than in catechesis. Catechesis builds on the germinal faith of the believer and nurtures that faith to grow into a transformative commitment of life. Catechetical instruction serves to deepen and nourish the faith, but it is always directed toward more than just gaining knowledge. Rather than just gaining knowledge, catechetical instruction seeks to form an identity. Showing how to live is a perfect description of teaching with this end in sight.

What does this ask, then, of the catechist? Speak from the heart. Offer the gift of yourself. Be ready to share why the teachings of the church are not just something to know but something to live by, and why they are something *you* live by. As witness, give evidence of your faith, and offer testimony. This need not always be a rousing and affective "witness talk." Rather, it is often the small anecdotes, the day-to-day examples, the concrete illustrations of the intersection of life and faith that allow people to discover and claim the same conviction in their lives. Invite people to listen more willingly by showing your passion, your conviction, and your enthusiasm for the faith as you teach its doctrines. In short, as Peter tells us: "Always be ready to give an answer for the hope that is within you" (1 Peter 3:15).

✸ *Questions for Contemplation*

- Recall the moment you first discerned your call to be a catechist. Why did you answer this call? What do you find most meaningful about your ministry?

- 1 Peter 3:15 says: "Always be ready to give an answer for the hope that is within you." How do you respond to this imperative? What is the answer for the hope within you?

- Recall again the person from your own religious formation whom you consider your best and most impactful teacher. What can you learn from this person for your own catechetical ministry?

■ What does a witness of sanctity mean to you? How in your life can you witness poverty, detachment, and freedom?

Prayer

Abba, our Father,
in the coming of your Son,
and in the sending of your Holy Spirit,
you give the gift of yourself to humankind,
a gift that calls us into ever-deeper relationship with you.
In our work of catechesis, inspire us
to become witnesses of this relationship,
and to give of ourselves generously to those
   you call us to serve.
Bless us especially when we are unsure
   or overwhelmed about how to begin
by sending your Spirit to animate us to teach your gospel
   by showing how to live it.
We ask this in the name of your Son, our Lord and teacher,
and by the power of the Spirit who breathes life
   into your church.
   Amen.

Must Love People:
A Ministry Animated
by Love

The work of evangelization presupposes in the evangelizer an ever increasing love for those whom he is evangelizing. That model evangelizer, the Apostle Paul, wrote these words to the Thessalonians, and they are a program for us all: "With such yearning love we chose to impart to you not only the gospel of God but our very selves, so dear had you become to us" (1 Thess 2:8; cf. Phil 1:8). What is this love? It is much more than that of a teacher; it is the love of a father; and again, it is the love of mother (Cf. 1 Thess 2:7–11; 1 Cor 4:15; Gal 4:19). It is this love that the Lord expects from every preacher of the Gospel, from every builder of the Church. A sign of love will be the concern to give the truth and to bring people into unity. Another sign of love will be a devotion to the proclamation of Jesus Christ, without reservation or turning back.

FROM PARAGRAPH 79, *ON EVANGELIZATION IN THE MODERN WORLD*
POPE PAUL VI, DECEMBER 8, 1975

The play *No Exit,* by the French philosopher Jean-Paul Sartre, offers a hard-hitting and challenging look at human interactions. In the play we meet three characters, Garcin, Inez, and Estelle, who find themselves locked together in a drawing room, which in fact turns out to be hell. They spend their time in shallow and self-absorbed conversation. At the end of the play, Garcin utters the line that has made this piece famous: "Hell is other people!"

This line is often quoted out of context to express our sense of frustration with others, or as an exasperated statement about the messiness of human relationships. In the context of the play, however, Sartre meant it not so much to disparage human relationships, but rather to show how hellish it can be when we perceive ourselves solely through the judgments and opinions of others. Garcin, Inez, and Estelle are particularly trivial and shallow in much of their conversation, and each in their own way is focused only on oneself. Their interaction shows us how frail self-identity can become when it is based on petty perceptions—whether ours or of those around us.

We all have days when we feel out of sorts with those around us. On those days we are irritable and impatient with people around us, who somehow do not fit into the box we imagined for that day's plans. On those days it becomes difficult to embrace the messiness of life and to be flexible to meet people where they are. On especially tough days we may come close to joining Garcin in his famous line, all the while skirting around Sartre's deeper meaning, by perhaps giving in to shallowness, pettiness, or self-absorption ourselves. Indeed, those days can be hellish, even in the context of ministry!

This chapter is meant as inspiration especially for "one of those days."

If Sartre's *No Exit* offers us a hard and unflinching look at the mess of the human condition, the above passage from *On*

Evangelization in the Modern World is its faithful, hopeful response. The antidote to self-absorption, pettiness, shallowness, and a weak sense of self is, of course, love. In another famous line, we are reminded: "Love is patient, love is kind. It is not jealous, it is not pompous, it is not inflated, it is not rude, it does not seek its own interests, it is not quick-tempered, it does not brood over injury, it does not rejoice over wrongdoing but rejoices with the truth. It bears all things, believes all things, hopes all things, endures all things. Love never fails" (1 Corinthians 13:4–8a). On "one of those days," this love is there and yearns to surround it all.

When it comes to sharing the Good News of Jesus Christ, the ministry of catechesis as a whole must love people. This is true in the practical, interpersonal sense as well as in the deeper sense of the ultimate meaning and purpose behind this ministry. How are we to approach and embrace this beautiful call to love in our own brokenness? How are we called to love on "one of those days"?

WHAT IS THIS LOVE?

On Evangelization in the Modern World poses this question and gives us two metaphors as it begins to respond to it: a love of a father and a love of a mother. Evangelizing and catechetical love is fundamentally parental. This parental love does not necessarily imply a certain age or a certain amount of power or authority. Instead, it calls the catechist to echo educationally what parents do biologically: to give life and to nurture it to grow. As a minister of the word, the catechist offers and nurtures life particularly through the sharing of the gospel in the context of religious education.

In the tradition of the church, we use the words "mother" and "father" in ways other than just to indicate biological parenthood. We address our priests as "Father" and women religious sometimes as "Mother" in addition to "Sister." These parental titles to celibate men and women reveal something important about their relationship with the church and with God's people. Through their vowed and consecrated life, they are called to be in a life-giving relationship with others, particularly the people they are called to serve. The idea of catechetical parenthood is somewhat similar to the spiritual parenthood of ordained and consecrated men and women. It is parenthood that arises from the life-giving power of the Word, Jesus Christ.

In the early centuries of the church, some men and women discerned a special way to express their faith. They moved away from their cities and into the desert wilderness and began to live the life of holy hermits, contemplating God's word in solitude. Even though these women and men sought the life of a hermit, others quickly began to seek them out to learn from their wisdom and example of holiness. Some seekers even settled nearby to remain close to these holy figures, who then became spiritual teachers to those who sought their words. Even though their hermitic life precluded them from biological parenthood, they became known as Desert Fathers and Mothers because of their life-giving words and lessons, which they offered to their seekers and disciples. Each word was like a seed planted in the heart of a seeker with the hope that it would grow into a robust faith.

In some ways, the catechist is called to imitate this life-giving relationship with others as centered on the Word. Instead of the desert wilderness, seekers come to the parish center, and instead of being a hermit, one is immersed in the busyness of parish life. The context is different, but the request is the same today as it was 1600 years ago: *Mother or Father, give me a good word!* In responding to the seeker with the life-giving word of the Good News, the catechist is a mother or father in faith.

Parents give and nurture life, but they also do this lovingly. What is this love? The love of a parent is self-giving, committed, total, and singular: it is all about bringing forth life to the fullest. It involves care, attentiveness, and presence but also direction and even discipline. It is about being responsible for life in the total sense of the term. In the context of catechesis the boundaries of this dynamic may be different, but the goal is the same: to show how to live the life of faith in a way that is self-giving, committed, total, and singular. The catechist is called to love in a way that helps to bring forth life to the fullest in the people he or she serves.

AN EVER-INCREASING LOVE

Recalling our chapter goal—to inspire us on "one of those days"—we know that, try as we might, the love we are able to give is not perfect. *On Evangelization in the Modern World* is aware of this. It does not call us to perfect love, but instead to a love that is ever-increasing. An ever-increasing love is like faith: it is a capacity for a committed and total self-gift that we grow into as we grow in our relationship with God. As Psalm 85 beautifully reminds us, love and faith are meant for each other: "Steadfast love and faithfulness will meet; righteousness and peace will kiss each other" (Psalm 85:10). We grow in each of these as we grow in our relationship with God.

Our relationship with God is fertile ground, especially for our capacity to love. As the First Letter of John tells us, "Beloved, let us love one another, because love is of God; everyone who loves is begotten by God and knows God. Whoever is without love does not know God, for God is love" (1 John 4:7–8). To grow in love, we need to grow in God. God is love, and the deeper our relationship with God, the deeper our capacity to love.

In his book *God Is Love*, Anthony J. Kelly reminds us about

30

the centrality of love in understanding who God is, how God relates to humankind, and what we are called to as believers. Love infuses all of this so much so that it is the very constitution of our reality of faith. Love at the same time surrounds and transcends us; it begins and ends in God. According to Kelly: "We are not saying 'love is God,' as though projecting a human notion onto God. Rather, 'God is Love,' in the sense that it is God who defines what love originally and ultimately means" (p. 8).

Kelly calls love God's self-revealing and self-giving action (p. 1). Each expression of these is a manifestation of love, whether the act of creation, the fidelity to the covenantal relationship with God's people, the fullness of God revealed in Jesus Christ, or the Spirit-led reality of the church. If self-absorption lands us in Sartre's hellish drawing room, self-gift and self-revelation invite us out of ourselves and into communion with others. On "one of those days," when all we want to do is crawl under our desk and hide away from others, the antidote to our misery actually is to seek to enter into communion with them more deeply.

In the beginning, Adam and Eve had one of those days too. They were living in paradise—PARADISE! Yet, deceived by the serpent, they both ate of the forbidden fruit and fell into sin. Immediately, as the first consequence of their action, their eyes were opened to the fact that they were naked; they felt shame and made clothes for themselves. Their initial impulse was to withdraw and distance themselves away from one another. Later in the day, when God walked through the garden, their impulse to separate deepened—they not only concealed themselves from one another, but they also hid from God! God called to them—called them back into communion—but they confessed the captivity of their nakedness, fear, and shame. After God laid out for them the consequence of their sin, we still find God's compassion and love embracing them: "the Lord God made garments of skins for the man and for his wife, and clothed them" (Genesis 3:21). Even in their willful separation, God reached out to them to literally clothe them in love.

In our own moments of hiding, we too are often held captive by fear, shame, regret, and feelings of being overwhelmed. Whatever forbidden fruits got us there and whatever the consequences that are ahead, God still calls out to us and is ready to stitch a garment to wrap around us. This garment of love covers and protects our woundedness so that our own love can emerge, increase, and become like a garment for the brokenness and woundedness of others.

A PROGRAM FOR US ALL

In Christian art, one popular image of Mary is that of Mother of Mercy. In this image, she is often depicted as surrounded by a great multitude of people, whom she gathers, covers, and shelters under her cloak. Mary, Mother of Mercy, helps us to think about the divine garment of love that God offered Adam and Eve, and how this now falls to the mission and ministry of the church.

Mary is our Mother of many titles. One of her most beautiful and important ones is Mother of the Church. As Mother of the Church, she is our most excellent member: her faith, her singular commitment, and her closeness to the Lord all show us what it truly means to be part of the body of Christ and to exist to share this reality with the world. As mother, she says yes to the Word and gives birth to, and nurtures, our faith. In this, she is the model for us in catechesis.

Mary's Mother of Mercy image helps to remind us that as the church, we too are called to gather, embrace, cover, and shelter people, and to do it with a mother's love. *On Evangelization in the Modern World* uses St. Paul's words to show this: *"'With such yearning love we chose to impart to you not only the gospel of God but our very selves, so dear had you become to us' (1 Thess. 2:8).*" It calls this tender, parental love *"a program for us all."* Whether it is God clothing Adam and Eve or Mary as Mother of Mercy gathering us under her cloak, we are given a model of a loving, tender embrace. This embrace cannot be merited: Adam and Eve receive it at their lowest, most undeserving point. Mary as Mother of Mercy shares with us her embrace only through the grace she herself has received from God. No one can earn this, but all are extended God's tender care. On "one of those days," when we are irked by or battling with our "problem people," the image of God's garment and Mary's cloak are powerful reminders of our call to love and to communion.

CATECHESIS CONNECTION

The work of catechesis unfolds in countless ways around the actual act of catechetical instruction. Even in the context of the catechetical classroom, content delivery is surrounded by the myriad social interactions that can either deepen or undermine the beautiful theological content that is shared. How we communicate in gesture, tone, and presence is an important and often overlooked part of what catechizes.

Of course, the work of catechesis is not just content presentation. It is scheduling and organizing sessions. It is making sure refreshments are set up and people receive hospitality before and after sessions. It is helping people submit forms and the appropriate paperwork. It is clarifying canon law and diocesan policy around sacraments. It is patiently journeying with those who are undecided, who miss important details and need to be reminded, who seem to not be taking the process seriously, or who do not yet have the language of faith to be able to express themselves comfortably. It is addressing questions that are sometimes obvious, thoughtless, or repetitious, and doing it gently, truthfully, patiently, and generously. It is especially in these contexts that we can find ourselves having "one of those days."

Human beings are messy and imperfect, and in this imperfect state we staff parishes, dioceses, ministry programs, and yes, even present ourselves to seek the sacraments or formation in a catechetical program. No one comes having figured sanctity out. As a result, we can either drive each other crazy unto crying "hell is other people," or we can insist on love. As with a garment that covers our woundedness and a cloak that gathers us in, God clothes us in love and calls us to clothe one another with the same tender care.

✹ *Questions for Contemplation*

- Recall the last time you were having "one of those days," especially in the context of your ministry. In retrospect, what do you see as your own woundedness? What part of you needed God to stitch you a garment?

- What is your understanding of love? How is God love? How has God's love been manifest in your life?

- Consider all that surrounds catechetical instruction and the myriad interactions you may have with the people you serve: forms, questions, scheduling, hospitality, etc. Where do you find it easiest to share Good News? Where is it the most challenging?

● *Prayer*

Divine Love,
you yearn to surround us with your tender care,
even in our sin and brokenness.
By the power of your love,
banish from our hearts any pettiness and frustration
that would otherwise drive us away from others
    and into our own self-absorption.
Fill us instead with a true spirit of self-gift so that we,
like our Mother of Mercy, might serve to gather your people
and embrace them in your love through our particular gifts
    in ministry.
We ask this in the name of your Son, who calls us
    to love one another as he has loved us,
by the power of the Holy Spirit.
Amen.

Centered *on* Christ: Our Primary *and* Essential Mystery

*In the first place, [Christocentricity] is intended to stress that at the heart of catechesis we find, in essence, a Person, the Person of Jesus of Nazareth, "the only Son from the Father...full of grace and truth" (John 1:14), who suffered and died for us and who now after rising, is living with us forever. It is Jesus who is "the way, and the truth and the life" (John 14:6), and Christian living consists in following Christ, the **sequela Christi**. The primary and essential object of catechesis is, to use an expression dear to Saint Paul and also to contemporary theology, "the mystery of Christ." Catechizing is in a way to lead a person to study this mystery in all its dimensions.*

FROM PARAGRAPH 5, *ON CATECHESIS IN OUR TIME*
ST. JOHN PAUL II, OCTOBER 16, 1979

While evangelization was the topic on the mind of the church in 1974–75, catechesis followed soon thereafter. In

1977, the synod of bishops, among them the cardinal from Krakow, Karol Wojtyla, gathered to think specifically about catechesis. Two years later, as Pope John Paul II, he distilled his reflections from the work of that synod into the apostolic exhortation *Catechesi Tradendae (On Catechesis in Our Time)*. *On Catechesis in Our Time* echoes the approach of *On Evangelization in the Modern World* in considering catechesis in the context of the church, reflecting on its content, beneficiaries, ways and means, method and spirit. In addition to offering description, it is a document that truly seeks to inspire: in its conclusion, the pope addresses all involved with the ministry of catechesis in a particularly inspiring fashion. The above passage comes to us from earlier in this document.

FINDING THE PERSON OF JESUS CHRIST

Have you ever sat with a lesson plan for your next session, thinking: "so much content, so little time"? Roman Catholic theology truly is a deep reservoir of intellectual thought, spiritual wisdom, and religious practice. There are centuries of history, layers of symbolism, multiple schools of thought, varied spiritual traditions, and a vast number of church documents to gather it all. It is impossible to exhaust a topic.

Coupled with this richness of content, we also have a shared sense that church teaching is very important. We look to the *Catechism of the Catholic Church* and other documents of the church to find the church's position on questions of faith, morals, and religious practice. We listen to the pope and our bishops to gather a sense of the Catholic position vis-à-vis contemporary issues affecting life and faith today. Our Catholic media oftentimes showcase apologetics—the defense of Catholic positions through systematic, reasoned debates. The content of the faith and its importance are all around us in the church.

Whether working with children or adults, knowing what the church teaches is one of the broad learning outcomes of any catechetical program. Knowing church teaching defined catechetical programs of old: pedagogy was structured around committing to memory clear and concise responses to key theological questions. In our present day, pedagogy may have shifted but the commitment to knowing content remains paramount.

Yet, the above passage invites us to take a step back and behold the bigger picture. The content of the faith is not ultimately *content*. It is in essence a Person, the person of Jesus Christ. All of the marvelous content of our faith is meant to lead, guide, and point toward him and to reveal him ever more fully. Just like evangelization is the church's identity, the Good News or content of our faith is found in the very being of Jesus Christ.

The content of faith as the person of Jesus Christ means understanding the role of church teaching in context. It means that each church teaching is important for what it actually teaches, but it is even more important for how it leads us ever deeper into encountering the person of Jesus Christ.

PEELING BACK THE LAYERS TO THE CORE

When I teach about this topic, I often use the example of the onion, just like the kind we all have in our pantries. Onions are ubiquitously important in cooking: a chopped and sautéed onion is the basis of countless soups, stews, casseroles, and other dishes. In Louisiana, onions are one third of the "holy trinity" of cooking, along with green peppers and celery. (If you add garlic, it's the "holy trinity and the pope.") Just like the importance of knowing what the church teaches in catechesis, onions in cooking are a given.

Onions are also a wonderful illustration of how church teaching exists in context. Cut an onion in half, and you will see dozens of concentric circles radiating from a core. Church teaching exists in a similar, concentric structure, with some doctrines closer to the core, with other beliefs and practices further out among the layers. All are part of the one onion, but they all exist in different relationship to the core and to one another.

If we peel the onion from the outside, it is impossible to get to the core without encountering all of the layers in between. In fact, each layer exists to protect and preserve the layer within it, until the layers come to the center. Church teaching is similar: each layer of teaching exists to protect, preserve, or help us better enter into the mystery of the inner core.

If you leave an onion in the pantry for too long, sometimes it will begin to sprout. A green shoot will emerge from its middle and grow long. If we cut the onion in half at this point, we will discover that the green shoot is coming from the very middle, the core of the onion. The core of the onion is where its life resides, it is from the core that the onion comes to life. This too is instructive for understanding church teaching—our central core, the very heart of it, is what gives everything else meaning and life. Of course, that very core is our belief in Jesus Christ, the *"Person of Jesus of Nazareth, 'the only Son from the Father...full of grace and truth' (John 1:14), who suffered and died for us and who now after rising, is living with us forever."* All church teaching exists to preserve, protect, and allow us to enter more deeply into this central core, this essential truth, which gives everything else around it its purpose and meaning.

Whether we are teaching about the Assumption of Our Lady, the various liturgical colors and seasons in the church year, the Rosary, novenas, *lectio divina*, patron saints, or why we have a pope and bishops, these and other questions like these all ultimately land on one same question: How does this teaching/practice help us better encounter the person of Jesus Christ? How does this teaching/practice invite us further into the inner core of our faith, the person of Jesus Christ? In this, catechesis is conscious of evangelization, conscious of always serving the sharing of the Good News of Christ, in every lesson and every session.

MEETING MYSTERY

As the passage above tells us, catechesis leads us to the mystery of Christ in all its dimensions. Returning to the moment of sitting with a lesson plan, this focus on the mystery of Christ begins to alleviate some of the pressure we may feel to fit everything in. Mystery gives us a sense of content that is not exhaustible, but rather continues to invite our consideration. We cannot fit mystery in, but we can pave the way for people to enter ever more deeply into it to meet Christ.

Mystery is a word that brings to mind secrets, detective stories, puzzles, and the unexplainable. It is a word that implies ambiguity, limited information, and lots of questions. When we call something a mystery, often it is a statement that means that something is not or cannot be fully known. Because of this, we accept mystery as fuzzy, and only a few persist in its ongoing investigation.

How can this word "mystery" apply to Christ, and to the central event of his being with us, the Paschal Mystery? Christ and his work are indeed unexplainable in some ways. Our response to him is based not on explanation but on faith, and "faith is the realization of what is hoped for and evidence of things not seen" (Hebrews 11:1). Faith moves as a response to being called forth by God; it is the human person responding to God's self-giving love that reaches out to us. Evangelization serves to facilitate such a faith response. In the context of catechesis, people present themselves for the process, having been so moved in faith but needing for that faith response to grow through instruction, prayer, and community. Catechesis starts with the mystery of faith.

The mystery of faith is important to keep in mind as our starting point. It means that all the instruction we offer ultimately folds into a complex and profound human-divine relationship that indeed cannot be exhausted in one's lifetime. As St. Paul tells us: "At present we see indistinctly, as in a mirror, but then face to face. At present I know partially; then I shall know fully, as I am fully known" (1 Corinthians 13:12). The role of instruction in this mysterious context is to support, nurture, and strengthen the faith response so that it continues on a dynamic path striving ever closer to communion with the Lord. St. Paul's vision offers a hopeful end to our striving: we shall see face to face; we shall know fully and be fully known. The end of our path of faith is to arrive into full communion with divine mystery. Catechetical instruction guides and nurtures faith so that we know the path and can remain on it. In this sense, our content is couched between mystery and mystery: the mystery of faith that responds to God's call, and the mystery of God unto eternity.

Christ is a mystery because the full meaning of him cannot be exhausted. At the same time, through faith, we are drawn into this mystery to enter into an ever-deeper relationship with him. In a more finite sense, human relationships function the same way. Spouses are ultimately a mystery to one another; even after years of marriage and even through profound experiences of intimacy such as the marital embrace, husband and wife are never fully known to each other. Part of the dynamism of the marriage relationship is discovering in a spouse something new, something unexpected and surprising, even after years of a shared life. We are mysteries to one another and delight in the fact that there is always more to know. Because of this, spouses are drawn to one another in this mutual discovery of one another's mystery.

In the Letter to the Ephesians, we read that this spousal

relationship is a fitting metaphor for understanding Christ's relationship with the church: "this is a great mystery, but I speak in reference to Christ and the church" (Ephesians 5:32). The "church" here, of course, is all the baptized, all who are members of his body. Thus, the mystery of an ever-deepening intimate relationship with Christ is something we are all called into. When grappling with how much content to include in a lesson, the question of "how do I present this topic so that it leads people into a deeper relationship with Christ?" is an essential one that guides us into mystery.

SEQUELA CHRISTI: FOLLOWING CHRIST

Entering into an ever-deeper relationship with Christ is not only a matter of gaining more knowledge about him. It is also about getting to know him by imitation of his example and by practicing his teaching. To meet the mystery of Christ, we must follow his example; the Latin phrase in the passage above for this is the *sequela Christi.*

Following Christ is both an exterior and an interior practice: it is both a spiritual disposition of obedience to him, and external actions that practice and show this commitment. In a sense, the *sequela Christi* helps to round out the task of catechesis to include not just instruction of content, but also engagement in prayer and spiritual practices, as well as in service and action. It is internal and external application of the content of faith in a way that the believer's life is transformed to resemble the life of Christ. To enter into the mystery of Christ means also this: to grow in the capacity to reveal Christ to those around us by word, deed, and witness of life. Following Christ, we become imitators of him so as to reveal him to the world. In this, catechesis comes to bear fruit and gives birth to evangelizers. Those whose initial faith catechesis nurtures into fullness become bearers of the Good

News. Those evangelized become evangelizers.

We noted above the phrase "Paschal Mystery." This phrase, the core of our understanding of faith, reminds us that the way of following Christ is not an easy task. It is the dusty roads of Galilee where feet get dirty; it is the rocky road where seeds die; it is a dangerous road where travelers get robbed and beaten. Yet it is also a road where feet are washed, where there is rich soil by the wayside, and where good Samaritans stop and come to the aid of those fallen. The road leads to Jerusalem, through an intense and cheering crowd, through the palaces of Herod and Pilate, through the city streets stumbling under the weight of a cross beam, to Golgotha, where Christ's feet, which have walked all these places, are brutally pierced and nailed to a cross. Yet the road will continue, and the risen Lord appears to walk them again, three days later, as he joins two travelers on the road to Emmaus, enkindles their hearts with the word, and reveals to them his presence in the breaking of the bread. How beautiful are the feet of those who bring good news! (See Isaiah 52:7; Romans 10:15.)

Before we were known as Christians, our ancestors in faith called themselves followers of the Way (Acts 9:2). Following the way of Christ is central to our identity. It means a life of self-gift offered in love on a road paved by the total reality of life, both broken and redeemed, messy and glorious, already and not yet. Catechesis prepares for this road and accompanies believers in walking it, together toward Christ, in all the dimensions of his mystery.

CATECHESIS CONNECTION

In the context of catechesis, seekers at times struggle with finding certainty as a necessary step before continuing on with the catechetical process. Seeking certainty can become a stumbling block for some, leading them to leave the process because of having questions or doubts about aspects of the content of faith. As part of the RCIA, the ritual process is structured so as to help seekers experience the transition from inquiry to firm commitment, culminating in the profession of faith offered just before baptism. Part of the task of catechesis is to help the seeker understand that certainty above all pertains to faith in Christ and readiness to make a commitment to him with one's life as part of the church.

Helping a seeker understand faith, mystery, certainty, and commitment can be a complex pastoral task. The emphasis above on the mystery of Christ certainly leaves room for unanswered and enduring questions and even moments of doubt in the life of the Christian. Abraham followed God's command and set out without knowing where it would lead, and yet he is called the father of faith. Mary said yes to God's word and likewise obeyed in faith while also posing the question to the angel: How can this be? These two examples show us supreme commitment to God in faith, while also allowing for growth in understanding.

The important catechetical task is to help a seeker understand how commitment in faith is possible even in the context of mystery. To be sure, intellectual clarity and correct understanding of church teaching are essential to help us wade into the mystery of God. Yet to truly embrace the truth of a teaching or to even understand the significance of a question sometimes takes years and the experience of living life in its ups and downs. Commitment to the faith means committing to the person of Jesus Christ and anticipating growth in understanding the content of faith as the truth of it unfolds in a person's life. It is a commitment that is certain about Christ, but willing to grow with the church in his mystery in all its dimensions. It is a certainty in the fact that one does not have all the answers but hopes for the fullness of truth in seeing God face to face.

✺ *Questions for Contemplation*

- Consider your favorite topic and its lesson plan. Examine the content you present. How does it engage the mystery of faith? How does it lead learners into the mystery of Christ?

- What does following the way of Jesus Christ mean to you?

- Pick a church teaching that you have had to explain in the context of catechesis. How does understanding this teaching lead one to the core of our faith, the person of Jesus Christ?

✺ *Prayer*

Mysterious God, though you are beyond our understanding;
you reveal yourself to us in the person of your Son,
   Jesus Christ,
who invites us into your divine mystery.
May the content of our faith always serve us
   to meet the person of Christ,
and may our faith, which you have enkindled
   by the power of your Spirit,
grow ever deeper as we walk the path of your Son.
May our teaching and ministry always guide
   and accompany those
whom you have also called to follow the Way.
We pray this through your Son Jesus Christ,
   by the power of the Holy Spirit.
Amen.

The Life-Giving Spirit *of* Catechesis

We wish to remind the entire Church that its first duty is that of evangelization. Our Predecessor, Paul VI, presented the directions for this in his memorable document: animated by faith, nourished by the Word of God, and strengthened by the heavenly food of the Eucharist, one should study every way, seek every means "in season and out of season" (2 Tim 4:2), to spread the word, to proclaim the message, to announce that salvation which creates in the soul a restlessness to pursue truth and at the same time offers strength from above. If all the sons and daughters of the Church know how to be tireless missionaries of the Gospel, a new flowering of holiness and renewal would spring up in this world that thirsts for love and for truth.

URBI ET ORBI ADDRESS
POPE JOHN PAUL I, AUGUST 27, 1978

John Paul I served as pope only for thirty-three days, from August to September of 1978. This short period leaves us only a handful of documents — mostly letters, speeches, homilies, and audiences. The above selection is from his *Urbi et Orbi* address, an inaugural message at the beginning of his pontificate in which he shared the vision that would have guided his service to the church.

John Paul I is affectionately called "The Smiling Pope" and was known for his warmth, approachability, and genuine delight in people. His audiences are replete with stories, anecdotes, and references to his own life experience. He has been upheld as a model for catechists for his ability to kindly embrace the audience and offer his teaching in ways they can best understand. He modeled this like a storyteller and often with children.

This above selection on evangelization was one of the six points of his "program" that he offered in his inaugural message. In it, he is committed to the vision of the Second Vatican Council and to the significant work of his predecessor Paul VI on the topic of evangelization. Coming from an exemplary catechist, his words on evangelization here are deeply inspiring but also challenging. His words call for an awakening, and they cast the work of evangelization in service to holiness and renewal.

CREATING A RESTLESSNESS OF SOUL

In calling us to evangelization, one section above is particularly eye-catching: *"to announce that salvation which creates in the soul a restlessness to pursue truth and at the same time offers strength from above."* A restlessness of soul—the quotation here offers this phrase in a unique light. Restlessness is a word we might associate with anxiety, being antsy, or lacking in a certain stability of the heart. We imagine a restless person pacing a room or flitting between one thing and the next, always looking for the next idea or task to alight on. Few of us would desire harboring such a sense of restlessness in our soul.

In lieu of a sort of spiritual anxiety, creating a restlessness of the soul in the context of Pope John Paul I's message suggests something else: an arousal or an awakening of the soul to the great and unfathomable mystery of God. It is a call resounding against spiritual slumber, a wake-up call inviting us beyond complacency and perhaps even drying up. It is a reminder that the gospel message never grows stale, and neither should our engagement with it.

A helpful analogy here is about two people falling in love. When a man and woman fall in love, there is a sense of wonder and delight in discovering the newness of the other—their life, their history, their hopes, joys, and sorrows. The two become present to each other as mystery: a mutual encounter that offers an enduring invitation to constantly know, learn, and love more. Lovers are literally drawn into one another in this beautiful dynamic, and there is also a type of restlessness found therein. The restlessness emerges from the sense of how much delight we have already discovered but also at the same time from sensing that there is so much more to know and to experience. The restlessness is a yearning for the more, as it carries us even more deeply into the relationship.

Such dynamism need not be reserved only for the beginning of a relationship, although it may often find its natural emergence there. In fact, couples who have been married for a long time know that the secret to the longevity of their relationship is to remain restless: to constantly seek into the mystery of the other person, to expect wonder, joy, and new discovery. In other words, a relationship grows if it is regarded as a dynamic reality, if we do not take it for granted, and we allow ourselves to behold the other constantly anew. This approach has a hospitality and freedom to it and an openness to the other as a complex, living, wondrous being.

When it comes to the gospel, John Paul I calls us to do the same. We must awaken our souls to recognize that our relationship with God is a type of falling in love. It is entering into a relationship that is eternal, inexhaustible, and filled with unending joy, wonder, and delight. Restlessness of the soul is the dynamism that draws us ever more deeply into this, and it is a movement animated by Holy Spirit. Our own spirit must seek and respond to this movement.

When it comes to the work of catechesis, we are called not only to embrace but to hand on this spiritual disposition, primarily through the way we expose learners to the Good News. We are called to announce salvation in a way that creates a restlessness of the soul to pursue the truth. This is offering catechesis in such a way that those present are at once filled and also hunger for more. Like a great conversation that expands well beyond it to reveal more directions, more questions, more pathways, catechesis of this sort comes to function like a portal to greater mystery. This mystery is not abstract ambiguity, but rather a grasping of truth that grows ever more profound, whole, and universal.

To offer catechesis in this fashion, it is important to be open to the Holy Spirit. As John Paul I's words emphasize, evangelization is called to create a restlessness of soul but also at the same time recognize the strength offered from above. The soul is stirred not for its own sake (or worse, to be disturbed) but so as to awaken to dynamism of the Spirit and to be caught up in this dynamism to be drawn into God. This means that both catechist and learner must grow in sensitivity to the Spirit through prayer and spiritual disciplines. Part of the task of catechesis is to instruct, model, and form the interior life along these lines.

HOLINESS AND RENEWAL

At the end of John Paul I's vision for evangelization is his belief that *"a new flowering of holiness and renewal would spring up in this world."* The language here evokes a garden where life is budding forth, flourishing, and bearing fruit. It is significant that he also plants holiness in this soil. As with the restlessness or dynamism of the soul, holiness too is intimately connected to the Holy Spirit. As *Lumen Gentium,* the Second Vatican Council's document on the church, instructs us, all are called to holiness, and the Spirit plays an essential part in this:

> The classes and duties of life are many, but holiness is one — that sanctity which is cultivated by all who are moved by the Spirit of God, and who obey the voice of the Father and worship God the Father in spirit and in truth. These people follow the poor Christ, the humble and cross-bearing Christ in order to be worthy of being sharers in His glory. Every person must walk unhesitatingly according to his own personal gifts and duties in the path of living faith, which arouses hope and works through charity. (LG 40)

It is the Holy Spirit that moves us and offers us the dynamism to follow Christ. Holiness in this sense is an ever-deepening conformity to Christ as made possible by graces of the Spirit, which are offered universally to the church, but also particularly to each of us as personal gifts. Through the Spirit, we are given the breath, the movement, and the ability to follow Christ, each in our way but also as one.

A new flowering of holiness implies a renewed openness to the Spirit, which produces, as a flower does, beauty, sweetness, and life. Considering the flower reveals it as a metaphor: it is made, in its color, nectar, and perfume, to offer an invitation. It is a living thing of hospitality that welcomes insects and birds so that new seed can form and new life can be conceived. In fact, in medieval spirituality, the bee was considered a symbol of the Holy Spirit. Thinking of spirituality in the shape of a flower and of holiness as a hospitality to the Spirit toward new life expands the notion of sanctity well beyond the ascetical life that we very often associate with it. Although ascetical practices compose a rich tradition and history, holiness fundamentally emerges from a posture of seeking the Spirit and striving to walk in step with the Spirit (Galatians 5:25). We all are called to this.

How do we seek the Spirit? One way is to recognize and honor the growth of life around us. In the medieval imagination, the created world revealed clearly the glory of God. Observing the growth and flourishing of living things communicated that God was at work, and this evoked wonder and praise. God's life-giving Spirit was at work everywhere. Saint Hildegard of Bingen, mystic and Doctor of the Church, recognized this profound connection between the growth of life and the presence of God, and called it *viriditas*—literally, greenness. God has greening power, the power to give and sustain life, so abundant that we cannot miss it in the natural world around us. In one of her mystical visions, St. Hildegard describes Divine Wisdom along these lines:

> I am the supreme fire and energy. I have kindled all the sparks of the living. I am the fiery life of divine substance, I blaze above the beauty of the fields, I shine in the waters, I burn in sun, moon and stars. And I awaken all to life with every wind of the air, as with invisible life that sustains everything. For the air lives in greenness (*viriditas*) and fecundity. (*THE BOOK OF DIVINE WORKS*, 1.2)

For St. Hildegard, this greening power of God was not reserved to just how the natural world comes to life. She rec-

51

ognized an integral connection between this and the mystery
of our faith. A composer of hymns, here is how she praised in
song the Virgin Mary:

> *O branch of freshest green*
> *O hail! Within the windy gusts of saints*
> *Upon a quest you swayed and sprouted forth.*
> *When it was time you blossomed in your boughs*
> *"Hail, Hail!" you heard, for in you seeped the sunlight's warmth*
> *Like balsam's sweet perfume.*
> *For in you bloomed so beautiful a flower, whose fragrance*
> *Wakened all the spices from their dried out stupor.*
> *They all appeared in full greenness.*
>
> **(O Viridissima Virga)**

The image of humankind as spices in dried-out stupor that return to greenness through the coming of Christ is a marvelous
one. It also echoes the call of John Paul I, above, to create a
restlessness of soul, a rousing from stupor to live life to the
fullest unto eternal mystery. The greening power of God gives
life to the natural world, but this also includes the human person and does so in our totality. God gives life to our world, our
bodies, and our souls. Recognizing and honoring life all around
and within us becomes an icon to divine mystery and a revelation of the work of God's Spirit. Holiness and renewal spring
up in our world when we begin to recognize God as author of
all life and live our own lives to honor and reveal our Creator.

THIRSTING FOR LOVE AND FOR TRUTH

God gives life. Every gardener knows that marvelous moment
of witnessing the tiny sprout when it first manifests above the
soil. Despite knowing well the biology of seeds and plants, the
transformation and appearance of the seed into sprout is al-

ways truly awesome. Here is a tiny life that was a dry seed only a short time ago. Of course, gardeners do not have time to stand by to marvel too long—the seedling needs to be watered, protected, and nurtured. It comes to life thirsting for more.

As Pope John Paul I states above, our world is thirsting for love and for truth. Part of the task of evangelization is to reveal this thirst for what it is. In our constant searching, consuming, and browsing, we are all living this thirst. We are made to seek more, but few among us have recognized the ultimate object of this. We look to quench our thirst with acquiring things or power or wealth or status. Sometimes we try to quench it with things that will consume us: food, drinking, drugs, dieting, exercise, sex, or reckless and risky behavior. Of course, we continue to thirst.

To thirst is to know we yearn for more. Christ himself thirsted; "I thirst" was one of his seven last words on the cross. Saint Teresa of Kolkata's memorable meditation on Christ's thirst reminds us that his thirst was not for water or for the sour wine on the sponge, but rather for each of us. Christ thirsts for each of us, and does so out of pure, total, and eternal love. This is the truth.

As evangelization reveals our thirst for what it is, the task of catechesis is to meet our thirst for more with the love and truth of Christ. Through catechesis we embrace our shared human desire for more, our thirst, and begin to quench it with love and truth, relationship and instruction, community and content. The two are always present and always in balance in good catechesis.

CATECHESIS CONNECTION

The quest for truth and its role in instruction reveal a special challenge in our day and time. Catechetical instruction is tasked with presenting and clarifying the truth, particularly as it is articulated in and through the teachings of the church. Catechists are therefore responsible for knowing clearly what the church teaches and how this teaching reveals the person of Jesus Christ, who is the way, and the truth, and the life (John 14:6). How should we go about this?

This poses a special challenge in our day because of a number of factors. In light of the postmodern transition of the twentieth century, our greater culture accepts as fact that truths are manifold and depend largely on one's perspective. What is true for me may not be true for you. Universal truths, applicable for all, are difficult to maintain with this mindset. Reality today is like a Picasso painting: simultaneously visible from many angles. This makes for an interesting, unexpected, but also fragmented image. How do we speak of truth in a context like this? For the church, the truth remains the truth: "Jesus Christ is the same yesterday, today, and forever" (Hebrews 13:8). At the same time, we are tasked with revealing Christ to a world that will consider the Good News as just one among a myriad of legitimate perspectives. It is important for catechists to discern this reality and seek the guidance of the Spirit along the way.

Perhaps in response to this postmodern mindset, there is also much energy in our church today around apologetics: being able to clearly articulate and defend the teachings of the church, especially through reasoned debate. Apologetics is passionate about the truth in its own way. In the context of catechesis, it can be energizing and enlivening for some, and many may come to seek catechesis because of having witnessed or heard powerful, inspiring apologetics. While apologetics may indeed enflame the faith in these ways, it is important to discern how to incorporate it into catechesis. Content must always find balance with relationship. We must speak the truth, but do so in love, so that "we should grow in every way into him who is the head, Christ" (Ephesians 4:15). Debating the teachings of the church may energize some but thoroughly intimidate others. Some will readily quote Biblical references while others are just beginning to find their confidence to speak about their faith at all. In addition, good questions and genuine discussion do not always mean that truth needs to be defended or debated. Conversations can also explore, deepen, celebrate, or experience the truth. As with the postmodern challenge above, good catechesis discerns and seeks the guidance of the Spirit for how to best serve the people gathered to seek truth and love.

⊛ *Questions for Contemplation*

- When do you experience a restlessness of soul in your spiritual life? What stories of Scripture, moments of liturgy, tradition, teaching, or experience rouse your soul from slumber? What calls you to seek deeper into mystery?

- How have you witnessed God's life-giving power? Where do you most yearn for renewal and flourishing?

- How do you balance truth and love in your catechetical ministry?

Prayer

Loving God,
You sent your Son to us as the way,
   and the truth, and the life.
We thirst for your love and truth,
   and yet quench this thirst
with things hollow, temporary, or harmful to us.
We find ourselves like dried up herbs and spices,
   essence dormant and just hanging on.
Send your Spirit, fiery life of your divine substance,
   to rouse us from slumber and
renew us to live life fully and eternally.
We ask this through your Son,
   by the power of the Spirit.
   Amen.

Catechesis *as a* Moment *of* Evangelization

*Catechesis cannot be dissociated from the Church's pastoral and missionary activity as a whole....Accordingly, while not being formally identified with them, catechesis is built on a certain number of elements of the Church's pastoral mission that have a catechetical aspect, that prepare for catechesis, or that spring from it. These elements are: the initial proclamation of the Gospel or missionary preaching through the **kerygma** to arouse faith, apologetics or examination of the reasons for belief, experience of Christian living, celebration of the sacraments, integration into the ecclesial community, and apostolic and missionary witness.*

Let us first of all recall that there is no separation or opposition between catechesis and evangelization. Nor can the two be simply identified with each other. Instead, they have close links whereby they integrate and complement each other.

*The Apostolic Exhortation **Evangelii Nuntiandi** of December 8, 1975, on evangelization in the modern world, rightly stressed that evangelization—which has the aim of bringing the Good News to the whole of humanity, so that*

all may live by it—is a rich, complex and dynamic reality,
made up of elements, or one could say moments, that are
essential and different from each other, and that must all
be kept in view simultaneously. Catechesis is one of these
moments—a very remarkable one—in the whole process
of evangelization.

FROM PARAGRAPH 18, *ON CATECHESIS IN OUR TIME*
ST. JOHN PAUL II, OCTOBER 16, 1979

For understanding the relationship between evangelization
and catechesis, the above-quoted passage is an essential one.
It comes from the "go-to" paragraph in the documents on
this question: *On Catechesis in our Time*, paragraph 18. It is
here that St. John Paul II identifies catechesis as a moment in
evangelization, and this description becomes normative and
much quoted elsewhere, including in the *General Directory for
Catechesis*. Let us pause with this passage to explore catechesis
as a moment of evangelization and as a process within a larger
ecosystem in the life of the church.

WHAT PREPARES FOR CATECHESIS
In a perfect parish, in an ideal diocese far, far away, seekers
present themselves for catechesis having experienced initial
evangelization in a way that has planted the seed of the Word
in their hearts. Their faith has been stirred, and they come
now ready to soak in the richness of the content of faith. They
bring their faith, like a seedling, to the process of catechesis
so that it can grow into a mature form and be nourishing to
them and to others.

In your actual parish and in mine, people arrive at the process of catechesis at various stages of faith. Some people come
to inquire, then disappear. Some inquire multiple times, mul-

tiple years, disappearing and reappearing along the way. Some come, but seem aloof, lukewarm, or obligated to be there. Some come with a faith so on fire that they could be teaching the sessions. Some are educated in the content of faith but are grappling with complex, challenging questions. Others know very little about the content of faith but just know they feel called to the Catholic Church. Some lack the confidence or ability to speak about their faith out loud; others speak readily and pray spontaneously. As you behold this multitude, how do you determine where to begin with them in the process of catechesis?

Ideally, catechesis builds on initial evangelization—it presumes some stirring of faith, some yearning for the More, some dynamism in the person to enter into deeper relationship with God. At the same time, the development of faith is less a linear process that moves neatly from point A to point B, like streaming water from a hose into a bucket. Instead, the development of faith moves more like a river: it is a dynamic and complex process that ebbs and flows, cycles back and forth in eddies, expands in tributaries and bayous, all the while flowing generally in one direction. As the catechist, where do you wade in?

On Catechesis in Our Time advises us to rely on "*the initial proclamation of the Gospel or missionary preaching through the* kerygma *to arouse faith, apologetics or examination of the reasons for belief*" as some of the ways that initial faith is enkindled in a person in response to God's call. At the same time, it is also possible that this initial proclamation, preaching, apologetics, or examination takes place simultaneously with the process of catechesis, the process of nurturing the faith response and educating for discipleship. As a later section of the document acknowledges: "In catechetical practice, this model order must allow for the fact that the initial evangelization has often not taken place....This means that 'catechesis' must often concern itself not only with nourishing and teaching the faith but also with arousing it unceasingly with the help of grace, with opening the heart, with converting, and with preparing total adherence to Jesus Christ on the part of those who are still on the threshold of faith" (CT 19). Considering all this, the catechist's job description has just grown to include in a significant way the role of "evangelizer."

In many ways, this is fitting. Not all evangelizers are catechists, but all catechists are evangelizers. This is true even if the people you serve have all perfectly received the initial proclamation of the gospel before coming to you for catechesis. Being an evangelizer emerges out of the font of one's baptismal vocation; catechesis, for those who assume this ministry, becomes one particular way of expressing this fundamental vocation. Being called to proclaim the Good News of Jesus Christ does not disappear with the call to the catechetical ministry; rather catechesis becomes a concrete way to continue living out this call. In this sense, the work of catechesis emerges from a basic evangelizing posture. In the context of catechesis, then, the ministry can always be shaped to reveal the basic foundation beneath it, which is to proclaim the Good News. Thus, instead of thinking of evangelization as another task of catechesis, it is always and already the task. The difference is in how close to this foundation the task of nurturing and educating for discipleship lies.

It is difficult to weave a one-size-fits-all garment to wrap around this. Balancing catechetical instruction with basic proclamation will depend on the unique set of people you are called to serve. It is also a matter of trusting in the context to proclaim the Good News in other ways: in your hospitality and in the hospitality of the team, in your tone and passion for the subject you are explaining, in the witness you and your team provide as persons of faith, and in the witness other participants provide as they too begin to articulate their faith journeys in the context of the discussions. God uses all of this to enkindle the heart of a person who is just on the brink of responding in faith.

Important also are the fruits of the Holy Spirit: love, joy, peace, patience, kindness, goodness, faithfulness, gentleness, and self-control (Galatians 5:22–23). When the communication of faith occurs in the context of catechetical instruction, it must be infused by these in order to manifest the fact that the Holy Spirit is at work. And if the Holy Spirit is at work, then we can trust that God is inviting the faith response of those present, no matter how dormant their faith is. We can also trust that authentic communication of the faith is not our own effort or fabrication, but rather it is always the work of the Holy Spirit, and at best, we can become faithful instruments through which the Good News may resound. When living the fruits as best we can, we are well on our way to becoming such a faithful instrument, and one that addresses the very faith of those present.

THE CATECHETICAL MOMENT

On Catechesis in our Time reminds us that the aim of evangelization is to *"bring the Good News to the whole of humanity, so that all may live by it,"* and catechesis exists as one remarkable moment within this broader, dynamic reality.

Using the language of moment is important. A person's relationship with God is lifelong and extends by hope unto eternity. The few months a person may spend as part of a catechetical process are truly a moment when compared to this. Although a moment by comparison, the opportunity for catechesis is nonetheless remarkable. It is a graced moment to receive instruction, to grow in understanding the mysteries of faith, and to engage in a communal process that aims toward truly appropriating the content of faith in one's life. This communal and intentional engagement with the content of faith is precious and yields an experience that studying and reflecting on one's own would not necessarily yield. Through the instruction of faith, catechesis communicates much more than its content. Catechesis offers the sense that the believer comes to belong somewhere, that he or she is participating in a process that will incorporate them as members of the body of Christ, or strengthen their role therein. It grants participants the sense that their presence, contribution, and witness of faith matter—that they are part of a community of faith. An independent study of the faith may be very enriching, but it does not communicate this important sense. Offering the sense of community is the unspoken gift of catechetical instruction, and it is the essential context that allows the content to yield its full meaning. Belief in God and belonging to Christ are always a communal matter, even if God calls forth our faith uniquely from each of us. Catechetical instruction cannot but reveal this essential fact: *there are people here who matter*. This simple statement is fundamental to our liturgy, to our morality and ethics, and to our understanding of church in the world.

In addition to this invaluable communal context, catechesis, of course, offers instruction. The exposition of the content of faith, done clearly, accurately, truthfully, and with passion, may be the first opportunity for many participants to hear what the Catholic Church actually teaches. In our North American cultural context, it is generally difficult to find a person who has never heard of Catholicism or who has absolutely no preconceived ideas about the Roman Catholic Church (generally difficult, but still possible). If a person presents himself or herself for catechesis, it is more than likely that they have some idea of what Catholicism is about, given that they are drawn to it enough to consider participating in catechesis. Participants generally arrive at the process with some framework for understanding Catholicism, the church, Christ, and God.

At the same time, the understandings people bring are partial, or can be replete with "immaculate misconceptions." This is simply the result of the generalized way that Roman Catholicism is presented in our greater cultural narrative, often told by people who are not theologically trained or who are part of a tradition of faith different from or even contrary to Catholicism. Popular ideas about papal infallibility, the role of the Blessed Virgin Mary, our relationships with the saints, and various assumptions about going to hell are just a few examples of what greater culture often accepts about Catholicism without considering our full teachings on these matters. People coming to catechesis may assume these and other ideas are correct, or have never had the chance to test their assumption and take a closer look at these. Catechesis is a remarkable moment because it may be the opportunity for many to hear the full truth of our teachings for the first time. In many ways, catechesis is the mechanism by which the misconceptions about Catholicism are undone, one person at a time.

Centuries ago, Saint Augustine of Hippo also grappled with the question of discerning the readiness of people presenting themselves for catechesis, and how to proceed with their instruction. His time was the fourth and fifth centuries, but some of his pastoral challenges were the same as those we face today. He too sought to introduce seekers to the true content of faith, especially when they came with misconceptions or erroneous assumptions. He was particularly concerned with people who came with openness to a kind of mysticism, turning to visions, dreams, and miracles to discern God's revelation. As he tells it, he strongly encouraged these seekers to begin with Scripture instead:

> His thoughts, however, ought certainly to be
> turned away from this line of things, whether
> miracles or dreams, and directed to the more solid
> path and the surer oracles of the Scriptures; so
> that he may also come to understand how mer-
> cifully that warning was administered to him in
> advance, previous to his giving himself to the Holy
> Scriptures. And assuredly it ought to be pointed
> out to him, that the Lord Himself would neither
> thus have admonished him and urged him on to
> become a Christian, and to be incorporated into
> the Church, nor have taught him by such signs or
> revelations, had it not been His will that, for his
> greater safety and security, he should enter upon a
> pathway already prepared in the Holy Scriptures,
> in which he should not seek after visible miracles,
> but learn the habit of hoping for things invisible,
> and in which also he should receive monitions not
> in sleep but in wakefulness. (ON THE CATECHIZING OF
> THE UNINSTRUCTED 6, PARAGRAPH 10)

For St. Augustine, introducing the concrete and true content of faith, beginning with Scripture, was paramount. In our day and time, it still happens that people become fascinated by miracle stories and supernatural occurrences surrounding our tradition. For example, the many apparitions of Our Lady have inspired countless people and drawn many more deeply to Christ and the church. (In some ways, Our Lady is the ini-tial evangelizer for many people!) And yet, to remain fascinat-ed solely by miracles and supernatural occurrences produces a faith that is something other than Roman Catholicism. As St. Augustine insists above: one "should not seek after visible miracles but learn the habit of hoping for things invisible." Hoping for things invisible is another way to define the substance of faith (Hebrews 11:1). Catechesis is the remarkable moment when one begins to learn the habit of faith, looking at the concrete ways God has revealed Godself to humankind: the person of Jesus Christ through the Scriptural word, as interpreted by the tradition of the church. This revelation is public, communal, and offered to all. It is the task of catechetical instruction to invite people into this public revelation, otherwise known as the content or deposit of faith.

That St. Augustine begins catechetical instruction with Scripture is important. Sacred Scripture is the fundamental place from where God's Word addresses us. It is a privileged place for the process of divine revelation: for God's communication to humankind. As St. John tells us in the beginning of his gospel: in the beginning was the Word, and the Word was with God and the Word was God (John 1:1). The role of the Word is also at the beginning of the story of Christ, as the angel Gabriel brings the Word to Mary, and Mary accepts the Word into her very body. Whenever God enters into relationship with humankind, the Word is there to address us. For this reason, beginning with Scripture is an indispensable start for the nurturing and instruction of faith in catechesis.

Christ himself modeled for us a way of catechesis on the road to Emmaus (Luke 24:13–35). After the resurrection he appears along this road and meets two travelers where they are, and he accompanies them. He hears their trouble and sorrow and responds by inviting them into Scripture, explaining it in a way that enkindles the hearts of the two as they walk with him. Their walk with the Scriptures leads them to the table where, finally, Christ reveals himself to them in the breaking of the bread. Overjoyed, they set out to share the good news of this encounter with others in Jerusalem. What is this story, if not an extended model for the process of catechesis, especially in the context of RCIA?

We begin with sacred Scripture to tell our story as truthfully, concretely, and authentically as possible. We also begin here because sacred Scripture reveals something essential about who we are, our identity as a community of faith. Sacred Scripture is like our family album, holding together the memories, stories, and snapshots of who we are. When we begin with sacred Scripture, it is a revelation of the Word, but also a revelation of the community of faith gathered around it. The moment of catechesis is the moment to invite a person into this story in a way that their own life story will be folded into it and transformed by it as well.

WHAT SPRINGS FROM CATECHESIS

In the story of the road to Emmaus one of the most important details is what the two disciples decide to do *after* having encountered the risen Lord in the breaking of the bread. According to St. Luke: "So they set out at once and returned to Jerusalem where they found gathered together the eleven and those with them who were saying, 'The Lord has truly been raised and has appeared to Simon.' Then the two recounted what had taken place on the way and how he was made known to them in the breaking of the bread" (Luke 24:33–35). Having heard the Scriptural word, and having encountered Jesus at the table, the disciples now set out at once to share the experience they have had with those who are still yearning to hear the Good News. The eleven and those who were with them had just witnessed the brutal execution of Jesus. They were grieving, their hopes dashed against the cross at Golgotha. In the midst of their grief, there was also new, unsettling information circulating: the tomb is empty; the body is gone. Some of the women who had gone to the tomb were reporting a wonder that had taken place. Peter who had also been there was processing it all, stunned and amazed. This was a group of people who needed clarity, who needed truth, and who, above all, needed healing in the midst of their grief. This is where the two disciples go to share their good news, which is in fact *the* Good News of Christ's triumph over death.

The two disciples of the Emmaus story are among the first examples we have of evangelizers. What is even more significant is that they are seekers who are turned into evangelizers through the amazing encounter they have with the risen Lord in sharing the word and at the table. In our present terminology, these are people who were catechized to become evangelizers. In the ministry of catechesis today, our goal is the same. From the catechetical moment flow a number of other moments in the life of faith. *On Catechesis in our Time* lists these as *"experience of Christian living, celebration of the sacraments, integration into the ecclesial community, and apostolic and missionary witness."* All of these have an evangelizing aspect to them, a way of revealing the fundamental Good News of Jesus Christ. The goal of catechesis is to enable a person so that his and her faith can be expressed through these other moments, and in a way that they become evangelizers and carriers of the Good News to those around them. Catechesis nurtures and instructs the faith response so that the believer can set out at once and run with the Good News to those who yearn to hear it most.

In the temporal realm, one of the chief aims of catechesis is making evangelizers. It is instructing and nurturing people with the content of faith so that their hearts will burn within them as they walk along the way. It is leading them to an experience of encountering the Lord in the context of the community that is his body. It is also extending them the invitation to moments beyond catechesis—experiencing the life of faith and sharing in the total life of the community, including its mission. In this, the moment of catechesis brings the believer full circle: from being evangelized to being the one who now engages in evangelization by word, deed, and witness of life.

CATECHESIS CONNECTION

We only have people for a moment. Making peace with this statement is one of the most important tenets of self-care in the context of the catechetical ministry. As we explored above, people present themselves for the process of catechesis from all over the faith-development spectrum. In addition to this, each person brings a unique personality, learning style, history, and set of personal or cultural experiences. If they decide to stay with us for catechesis, we must acknowledge that this opportunity, albeit a remarkable one, is only a moment of their overall journey of faith. We must trust that God has led them to this point and that God will continue to lead them beyond what our catechetical ministry can offer.

If our approach is that this moment is the one and only opportunity a person has to grow in their faith, this assumption can lead us astray. This leads us to feel undue pressure to fit in as much as possible, to engage the person as much as possible, and to present every opportunity possible along the way. Although doing the best we can for each person is a laudable standard, we can overdo it, especially as we begin to think of ourselves and our ministry as the only opportunity for grace in a person's life. That is a lot of pressure.

We must also ponder where this approach might leave room for God, other than through us. St. Teresa of Avila's famous prayer tells us that "Christ has no body now but yours," but this does not mean that it is only *your* body, hands, and feet, and no one else's. At the end of the day, catechesis is trusting in God and returning to God all the seeds planted through our work so that *God* can now bring them to life. This trust and release is the catechist's act of faith and acknowledgment that our work is from God and for God, and that it is animated by God. We are workers in the vineyard. Keeping in mind that catechesis is but a moment reminds us of this perspective and gives us freedom to continue to do our work with joy, purpose, and faith.

✸ *Questions for Contemplation*

- Think about a typical lesson or session you lead, and the many ways you communicate the content of faith therein. Think about what you communicate explicitly in teaching, and what you communicate implicitly by your presence, interactions, gestures, tone, hospitality, and facilitation of the group. Where do you see the potential for evangelization in what you already do? What can you do better?

- What role does sacred Scripture play in your catechetical curriculum? In what ways can you create more opportunities for seekers to be addressed by the Word?

- If one goal of catechesis is to transform seekers into evangelizers, what impact does this have on catechesis? What can you do differently with this goal in mind?

Prayer

Eternal God,
you reveal yourself to us most fully
in the incarnation of your Son, Jesus Christ,
who is the Word Incarnate.
Inspire us to serve him,
so that catechesis might truly be a ministry of the word,
and a moment in which the response of faith deepens
and expands through our work of instruction and nurture.
Send us your Spirit so that the people we serve in catechesis
may be led in truth and clarity into the content of faith,
and that their hearts will burn as they meet you there.
By your Spirit, may we all become joyful
    and urgent messengers of your Good News.
We ask this in the name of your Son,
    by the power of the Holy Spirit.
Amen.

Communicating
the Word *of* God

The *immense horizons of the Church's mission and the
complexity of today's situation call for new ways of
effectively communicating the word of God. The Holy
Spirit, the protagonist of all evangelization, will never fail
to guide Christ's Church in this activity. Yet it is important
that every form of proclamation keep in mind, first of all,
the intrinsic relationship* **between the communication of
God's word** *and* **Christian witness**. *The very credibility
of our proclamation depends on this. On the one hand, the
word must communicate everything that the Lord himself
has told us. On the other hand, it is indispensable, through
witness, to make this word credible, lest it appear merely as
a beautiful philosophy or utopia, rather than a reality that
can be lived and itself give life. This reciprocity between
word and witness reflects the way in which God himself
communicated through the incarnation of his Word.
The word of God reaches men and women "through an
encounter with witnesses who make it present and alive."
In a particular way, young people need to be introduced to
the word of God "through encounter and authentic witness*

*by adults, through the positive influence of friends and the
great company of the ecclesial community."*

PARAGRAPH 97, *THE WORD OF THE LORD* (*VERBUM DOMINI*)
POPE BENEDICT XVI, SEPTEMBER 30, 2010

In the 2010 apostolic exhortation *The Word of the Lord* (*Verbum
Domini*), Pope Benedict XVI gathered the wisdom gleaned
from the 2008 synod of bishops. That year's theme was the
"Word of God in the Life and Mission of the Church." *The
Word of the Lord* is a rich and comprehensive treatment of this
theme, and it devotes some of its attention to evangelization
and catechesis. Evangelization and catechesis, fundamentally
called ministries of the word, both find deeper meaning when
considered as rooted in the Word and existing in service to it.
Communicating our words in service to the Word fully and
with integrity is indispensable when it comes to catechetical ministry. This is also at the heart of evangelization: the
sharing of the Good News is essentially a communicative act,
whether done through proclamation, teaching, preaching, or
the actions and witness of one's life. Most basically, catechesis
and evangelization are engaged in the communication of the
faith. This chapter invites us to rediscover the relevance of
communication in the sharing and nurturing of faith.

NEW WAYS OF COMMUNICATING

The quoted selection from *Verbum Domini* begins with acknowledging the dynamic reality of our times. We are called
to the task of communicating the faith *effectively*: this means
that the communication of the message must be carried
out in a way that it is fully received, understood, and lived.
Communication of this sort genuinely speaks to the reality
of our times and offers its message in ways that people can

understand. In the spirit of the Second Vatican Council, this calls for becoming literate in reading the signs of the times and becoming effective translators of the gospel message so that it can resound as fully as possible for our day and time.

Effective communication involves an outward movement that seeks to engage another: it is a relational act. This means that both the sender and receiver of the message are engaged in the activity of communication. The sender makes an effort to put forth the message clearly and comprehensibly for the receiver, and the receiver offers the disposition of listening and welcoming the content for consideration. At the deepest level, both sender and receiver are engaged in an act of self-gift. In putting forth a message, the sender couples this with a genuine intention to share himself or herself, while the receiver, in the disposition of listening, offers her own hospitality as part of the act of communication. Communication is so much deeper than the sharing of information. At its most profound level, it is the giving of oneself in love (*Communio et Progressio,* On the Means of Social Communication [1971], 11). Effective communication, then, is always aware of this relational, human dynamic at its heart.

Effective communication in our times also brings to mind the digital culture in which we find ourselves. Indeed, the quotation above refers to new ways of communicating in service to the Word, which in our day inevitably imply social media, apps, and increasingly advanced electronic gadgets. However, Pope Benedict's focus on new ways here refers to another important cultural reality: people who have grown lukewarm in their faith or have lost interest altogether; people who are "baptized but insufficiently evangelized" (VD 96). His call for new ways builds on the consistent concern of St. John Paul II for sharing the gospel anew, with new ardor, new methods, and new expressions. His call is for a new evangelization.

The new evangelization is an expression that has received much attention in recent years. For St. John Paul II, this theme echoed throughout his ministry, beginning in the late 1970s. Pope Benedict continued in this vein, and in 2012 he made the new evangelization the topic of the synod of bishops gathering that year. The new evangelization is essentially communication of the gospel that takes into consideration the reality of our time and seeks a more effective way to engage with people today. In some ways we can argue that this has always been the task of the church, and wonder what is new about it.

The novelty of the new evangelization is its intentional focus on the *ongoing* challenge of sharing the Good News. Many people who have received the sacraments and who perhaps practiced their faith at one point no longer do so. Their cases present a puzzle for the established pattern of initial evangelization followed by catechesis, followed by a robust participation in the community of faith. In the case of many people, that initial faith response, nurtured in catechesis, has now become withered and rests dormant. Their participation in the community of faith may be perfunctory, infrequent, or non-existent. To reawaken the faith, a new and rousing experience of evangelization is needed before offering the nurture and instruction of ongoing catechesis. This reality also calls us to broaden the context of catechesis considerably beyond sacramental preparation or to approach sacramental preparation in a more comprehensive and lifelong way.

The new evangelization calls us to reconsider evangelization as something that may need to be extended and re-extended over a lifetime, even if a person has already been catechized and has received the sacraments. The beauty of this reconsideration is that we can find ourselves included in this as well. The gospel message seeks to address all of us anew, each day, whether we are newborns in the faith or seasoned disciples. We never graduate from being addressed by the gospel. For ministry professionals, this is indeed healing and beautiful. We ourselves are recipients of the gospel—not just decades ago, not just when we were first moved to respond to the Lord in faith, not just during our formation and training, but today, here and now. We each have parts within ourselves that yearn for the Good News, whether we are a seasoned teacher of the faith or a person encountering the Lord for the first time. The new evangelization allows us, the evangelizers, to continue to be evangelized ourselves by the Good News, no matter how "experienced" we are in the life of faith. In order to evangelize, we must be evangelized and remain open to both of these in tandem.

The new evangelization also takes seriously the reality of people who have grown dormant in their faith. Some people may have never had the opportunity to claim an adult faith—a mature relationship with God that engages their will, intellect, and life circumstance. Catechized as children, they perhaps lost the sense of engagement with the community of faith while navigating through youth and young adulthood. Now, as adults, communal faith and religious practices are infrequent or no longer a part of their life at all. Instead, these have been replaced by secular narratives as ultimate means of making sense of life and the world around us. How can the gospel speak specifically to their lives in these circumstances? With abundant joy, fulfillment, and deeper meaning.

Others may have a different story. Raised and catechized in the faith, they may have experienced a crisis in a way that their understanding of faith was not able to adequately address. A tragedy made them question an all-loving and just God. A crime, addiction, or abuse made them wonder if God indeed is good and merciful. A negative interaction with clergy, religious, lay ministers or even members of the community led them to dismiss the church as a deeply flawed institution. As a result, they no longer participate in the community of faith or engage in religious practices. How can the gospel speak specifically to their lives in these circumstances? With healing, hope, and compassion.

Others still may experience a crisis of a different sort. They may struggle and even disagree with a particular teaching of the church, whether concerning sexual morality, the dignity of life, divorce and remarriage, or issues around gender. They have been catechized and have practiced the faith, but some such issue has become a stumbling block. Perceiving themselves as "judged," they grow apart from the community of faith and possibly from religious practices altogether or perhaps seek out another ecclesial community or religion. How can the gospel speak specifically to their lives in these circumstances? With truth, mercy, and reconciliation.

In this fashion, the new evangelization seeks effective communication from a fundamentally relational starting point. It is the Good News addressed particularly to people of our time, taking seriously their hopes, joys, challenges, and deepest questions. Still embracing those who have never been evangelized, the new evangelization also extends an arm along these lines to those no longer participating in the life of faith as well as to those who do. Speak, Lord, for all of us yearn for your Good News.

WORD AND WITNESS

When calling for effective communication in new ways, Pope Benedict, above, places important emphasis on the connection between word and witness of life. As he states: "*On the one hand, the word must communicate everything that the Lord himself has told us. On the other hand, it is indispensable, through witness, to make this word credible, lest it appear merely as a beautiful philosophy or utopia, rather than a reality that can be lived and itself give life."* For the catechist this implies an intimate familiarity with God's Word, especially as encountered through sacred Scripture.

Sacred Scripture is far more than just an artifact of collected writings. It is a point of encounter with the living God, who speaks and listens to our questions (VD 4). At the 2012 synod of bishops, the text of the Bible was placed in the center of the assembly hall to remind them of this. The Word of God is living, and enters into our concrete reality as God's self-communication to humankind. The Word addresses us relationally; it is effective communication par excellence. We recognize Christ as the Incarnate Word, God's self-communication extended to us so intentionally that it becomes flesh to dwell among us. Christ's communication is self-gift to the highest degree, and he desires and calls forth our response. It is communication fully addressed to our reality and offered in a way we can best understand. In turn, we are called to a posture of hospitality, and to authentic listening to welcome the Word. This beautiful dynamic of divine-human communication is made concrete for us in sacred Scripture, as one profound way to enter into this mystery. In the life of the church, sacred Scripture is proclaimed, read, sung, heard, and received to underscore this. The church thus invites us into the prayerful experience of welcoming and listening to the Word and allowing it to engage us and call forth our faith. In the liturgy, it is by no accident that the proclamation of the word and preaching is followed by the Creed. Addressed by the Word, we listen and respond in faith.

Intimate familiarity with the Scriptural word is a must for catechesis. As we find in the Second Letter to Timothy: "All scripture is inspired by God and is useful for teaching, for refutation, for correction, and for training in righteousness, so that one who belongs to God may be competent, equipped for every good work" (2 Tim 3:16–17). Teaching, refutation, correction, and training in righteousness read like a job description of a minister of the word, another term describing the work of evangelization and catechesis. The ministry of the word is about communication: it is the church's specific work for transmitting God's self-communication to humankind. It is the divine Word shared in human words by the work of the church (*General Directory for Catechesis*, 50). Primary proclamation, catechesis for initiation and for continuous education, liturgy, and theology are some of the basic ways the church carries out the ministry of the word. Catechesis as a ministry of the word must therefore remain rooted in the Word to authentically contribute to this greater ecclesial task.

What does it mean to be rooted in the Word? This expression speaks of stability and having a source of life. To be rooted means to have a firm and secure foundation, as well as the opportunity to grow and flourish from this. To recall Pope Benedict XVI, it means absorbing the Word so it can be lived and itself give life. To be rooted in the Word is more than a sterile repetition of the biblical word. Rather, it is a total communication of the Word in a way that shows it matters; it is communication of the Word showing how it has given one life. In other words, it is witness.

To become a witness of the Word means that one has such intimate familiarity with it that the Word can be revealed to others through one's life. Becoming familiar with the Word involves listening to, embracing, and living it. It means freeing our understanding of the Word from being an artifact and recognizing it instead as the self-gift of the Living God. Practically, it involves attentive presence to the Word in the liturgy and in one's prayer life and study. Praying the liturgy of the hours, meditating on the lectionary readings, engaging in *lectio divina*, or participating in a Bible study are some intentional practices for gaining intimacy with God's Word. Welcoming the Word through such practices is transforming. It is welcoming the Word of God to speak in our lives and through our lives. By this, we begin to reciprocate God's self-gift by offering ourselves in return to allow God to speak to others. Through this, we become true receivers of the Word and truly in communication with God.

HOLY SPIRIT, PROTAGONIST

In the earliest days of the church, a group of disciples huddled in an upper room while a festival was unfolding around them in Jerusalem. They were praying, for they had been told by Jesus to wait for the promise of the Father, the Holy Spirit (Acts 1:4–5). On Pentecost day, the Spirit arrived with tongues of fire and rushing wind and filled each of them in a mysterious, powerful, transformative way. What happened next was communication that surpasses our understanding. The Spirit gave each of them the astounding ability to speak in foreign languages, enabling communication with all the people gathered in Jerusalem for the festival. Then Peter got up and gave the most powerful, eloquent speech of his life. Three thousand were baptized after hearing him. As a conclusion to this scene, we get a glimpse of the apostolic community, the perfect prototype of the church, in which all share in the communal life of teaching, worship and prayer, and care for those in need. In this second chapter of the Acts of the Apostles, the Holy Spirit is the protagonist who transforms a group of disciples into the church, and does so through a miracle of communication.

Pope Benedict XVI tells us that *"the Holy Spirit, the protagonist of all evangelization, will never fail to guide Christ's Church"* in the effective communication of the gospel message. This is a fact: whenever the authentic communication of the faith is taking place, it is the work of the Holy Spirit. It is the Holy

Spirit who gives us the ability to speak, the very breath that allows us to share the message in a way that people can understand. The Holy Spirit is the source and power behind the dynamism that propels the gospel forth *and* that engages the hearer to receive it in faith. To communicate more effectively, we must grow more sensitive to the Holy Spirit and open ourselves up to the Spirit's prompting, gifts, charisms, and fruits. More broadly, this implies greater attentiveness to our own spirituality, and to hone this capacity we have to became more aware of, sensitive to, and tuned into God's presence. God is present always and everywhere, but are we aware? Do we hear and recognize the voice of the Shepherd so that we can follow?

Saint Benedict of Nursia, the sixth-century monastic with an invaluable spiritual legacy, was especially attentive to prayerful listening as essential for the life of faith. He famously begins his Rule with "Listen, my son, to the master's instructions, and attend to them with the ear of your heart." For St. Benedict, listening is more than just hearing or paying attention to what is heard. It is a spiritual disposition and a posture of receptivity to the Word of God, which can address us from expected and unexpected places. Monks will encounter the Word in their communal prayer, in their holy reading, in the teaching of the abbot, in their rule of life, in their fellow monks, but also in the guests or strangers arriving at the monastery, "who are to be welcomed as Christ" (The Rule of Benedict, 53:1). From all of these sources, God may speak. Benedictine monks and nuns are committed to obedience to the Word and to offering hospitality, which is above all a prayerful commitment to listening always to the Word with one's heart, with one's very core.

For perfecting this posture of prayerful listening, Benedictines spend a significant amount of their time with holy Scripture. Their regular practice of daily prayer comes mostly from the psalms, as well as other Biblical readings. In addition to this, the Rule of St. Benedict commits them to the practice of *lectio divina*, a slow and prayerful way of reading the Bible. St. Benedict himself, as he writes the Rule, peppers his explanations throughout with quotations from the Bible. He does this so seamlessly that one can readily imagine how intimately he knew the Bible, and how much the biblical word became his own vocabulary. All this is an integral foundation for listening to God, attentiveness to the Spirit, and being able to communicate the faith effectively in word and witness of life.

Along these lines, Pope Benedict XVI follows the above-quoted passage from *Verbum Domini* with the following:

> There is a close relationship between the testimony of Scripture, as the self-attestation of God's word, and the witness given by the lives of believers. One implies and leads to the other. Christian witness communicates the word attested in the Scriptures. For their part, the Scriptures explain the witness which Christians are called to give by their lives. Those who encounter credible witnesses of the Gospel thus come to realize how effective God's word can be in those who receive it. (VD 97)

Evangelization, old or "the new," begins not with an outward movement but rather an inward one. In the story of Pentecost revisited above, we often focus on the rush of wind and tongues of fire and miss the quiet, prayerful waiting that preceded it. In order to take part in the powerful and amazing movement of the Spirit that communicates the faith, we too must first turn inward and learn to listen with the ear of the heart. As Pope Benedict XVI teaches, Scripture has an indispensable role in this. Scripture also offers a bridge that moves us out of ourselves to community, to serve those who are yearning for the Word again or for the first time.

CATECHESIS CONNECTION

Because evangelization and catechesis are so closely connected, discussions of the new evangelization naturally prompt the question of whether there might also be a new catechesis. If the new evangelization recognizes the ongoing need for the proclamation of the Good News for all, then catechesis can also imagine broader ways to engage in the ongoing formation of the faith.

What would a new catechesis include? What would be its new methods and new expressions? These are exciting questions that in and of themselves reveal the stirrings of the Holy Spirit. One way to begin imagining this is to revisit catechesis as both initiatory but also ongoing formation, and to think intentionally about what ongoing formation can look like, especially for those who may have grown lukewarm or disinterested altogether. What are the best ways for catechesis to begin to speak to the reality of people's lives, whether that reality involves apathy, loss of meaning, alienation, hurt, or exclusion? What ongoing formation can best nurture the fragile seedling of hope, possibility, or deeper meaning that a new evangelization brings forth in these lives?

Another way is to think about the connection between catechesis and the liturgical life of the church and to imagine ways that catechetical instruction could prepare people for liturgical moments other than baptism, confirmation, or first communion. How can we catechize for the ongoing reception of the sacrament of reconciliation? How can we catechize for the anointing of the sick? (Still perceived by many as last rites, our hospital and hospice chaplains will thank catechists for this!) How can we catechize for other rituals, such as the renewal of baptismal promises, the veneration of the cross, Lenten and Advent practices, processions on Holy Thursday or Corpus Christi, or the singing of sequences on Easter or Pentecost? Or, more basically, how can we catechize for the Creed, the Lord's Prayer, or understanding the Scriptures? The new catechesis in all of these is intentionally recognizing that our learners may be people who are lifelong Catholics and who have otherwise received their sacraments and have been part of the community of faith to greater or lesser degree. The challenge of this new catechesis is to reveal such formation "purposelessly," or, in other words, done for its own sake, not for fulfilling a process or "getting" a sacrament. There is great potential here for building on the new evangelization of those already active in the church.

Yet a third way to think about the new catechesis is the media by which catechesis is offered. Good catechesis is always conscious of handing on the faith as content but also as relationship with the church; the communal experience and context matters significantly alongside the total and comprehensive teaching of content. Holding these two in balance becomes all the more important today, as we find ourselves in a digital culture. So much content *about* the faith is available online, but is this necessarily the same as the content *of* faith? Likewise, social connections abound, but are these authentic experiences of community? Perhaps yes, perhaps no. It is important to discern these questions and to recognize digital culture as an important puzzle piece in the overall picture of communicating the faith. The call for new methods and expressions of the faith certainly invite us to examine the language, values, and traditions proper to digital culture, and to recognize the importance of communicating the faith in ways that people today can understand. This may mean establishing a presence on social media, but it also means discerning how our use of technology reveals some bigger questions about human life, what hopes, joys, or brokenness are most manifest in digital culture, and how the gospel can speak to all of this. Come, Holy Spirit.

✸ Questions for Contemplation

- What does effective communication look like? Recall an example when something important was effectively communicated. How did the sender and receiver contribute to this experience? What can this teach us for catechesis?

- What role does Scripture play in your own spirituality? What connection is there for you between Scripture, effective communication of the Word, and witness of life?

- In what ways is catechesis a ministry of the Word? How can this become more explicit in what you do?

- What would you include in a new catechesis that follows from the new evangelization?

✪ *Prayer*

Eternal God,

you sent your Son into the world

spoken to us as the Word Incarnate,

spoken to us in the best way we can understand.

We praise you for your divine self-gift

that addresses us so intimately

and ask you to shape us in the image

   and likeness of your Son

Jesus Christ the Perfect Communicator,

   especially as we seek

to serve you in the ministries of your word.

Send us your Spirit again to give us the ability to speak,

to enflame in us that Pentecost spirit that leads

to the gathering of your people into one.

We ask this in the name of Jesus Christ, Word Made Flesh,

by the dynamic power of the Holy Spirit.

Amen.

8

Catechesis *and* *the* Way *of* Beauty

*Every form of catechesis would do well to attend to the "way of beauty" (**via pulchritudinis**). Proclaiming Christ means showing that to believe in and to follow him is not only something right and true, but also something beautiful, capable of filling life with new splendor and profound joy, even in the midst of difficulties. Every expression of true beauty can thus be acknowledged as a path leading to an encounter with the Lord Jesus. This has nothing to do with fostering an aesthetic relativism which would downplay the inseparable bond between truth, goodness and beauty, but rather a renewed esteem for beauty as a means of touching the human heart and enabling the truth and goodness of the Risen Christ to radiate within it...Each particular Church should encourage the use of the arts in evangelization.*

FROM PARAGRAPH 167, *THE JOY OF THE GOSPEL*
POPE FRANCIS, NOVEMBER 24, 2013

It is difficult to select just one inspiring passage from Pope Francis' apostolic exhortation *The Joy of the Gospel (Evangelii Gaudium)*. In this document Pope Francis thinks further with the work of the 2012 synod of bishops on the new evangelization. Called the blueprint for Pope Francis' plan for guiding the church, *The Joy of the Gospel* is full of memorable passages and vivid metaphors: "there are Christians whose lives seem like Lent without Easter" (6); "an evangelizer must never look like someone who has just come back from a funeral" (10); "a tomb psychology develops and slowly transforms Christians into mummies in a museum" (83); and "I prefer a Church which is bruised, hurting and dirty because it has been out on the streets, rather than a Church which is unhealthy from being confined and from clinging to its own security" (49). These are just a few among the inspiring and challenging words of Pope Francis in this document.

The selection above is perhaps less quoted than these memorable phrases, but it nonetheless is profound and inspiring. In it Pope Francis calls us to think about beauty and its role in drawing a person closer to Jesus Christ.

BEAUTY, GOODNESS, AND TRUTH

Pope Francis presents beauty as inseparably bound to goodness and truth. This already offers us a clue that beauty is more than what pleases the eye. Beauty, goodness, and truth are together called the "transcendentals" and have a long history in philosophical thought. (Classically, these qualities include a fourth: unity.) Catholic theology has long considered these as qualities related to what we imagine to be the highest form of being, and they are also qualities that all beings share in common. In other words, these qualities suggest a bond between all beings and the Ultimate Being, God. Pondering these three invites us into a profound sense of communion. Beauty, goodness, and truth also are intimately interrelated. Beauty reveals goodness and truth; goodness reveals truth and beauty; and the truth is good and beautiful. Leave one of these out, and these become ends in themselves rather than a quality revelatory of something more.

As Pope Francis tells us above, *"a renewed esteem for beauty is a means of touching the human heart and enabling the truth and goodness of the Risen Christ to radiate within it."* Beauty stops us in our tracks, it rouses us from our mundane stupor and from the daily grind of going through the motions of life to the point of becoming tired and disillusioned with it all (or, in Pope Francis' words, "tomb psychology"). Beauty compels us to stop, take notice, and allow ourselves to be moved beyond the mundane. Beauty is a wake-up call to the more, or what is called the *magis* in Ignatian spirituality. It touches the heart and moves us to awe, to contemplation, and to a renewed sense of abundant life. Saint Ignatius of Loyola, while seated on the banks of the Cardoner River, had an amazing mystical experience like this; it was a moment that became decisive for his life. By the Cardoner, he saw all things as if for the first time.

Beauty also makes way for goodness and truth; once we open up to the contemplation of beauty, we can truly experience goodness and discover truth. Experiencing goodness means not just recognizing something good that happens to us; it means a conscious awareness of goodness that calls us beyond the experience to ponder its Source and to evoke from us awe and gratitude. We discover truth as we recognize goodness—as a grace, a gift of God's self-surrendering love. The risen Christ radiates in our hearts when we behold this mystery and give ourselves over to it in return. Another word for this is the response of *faith*.

Because beauty, goodness, and truth can help move us to faith, these qualities become all the more important in evangelization and catechesis. They are not just lofty concepts of philosophy and theology, but rather wisdom about the human heart and its transformation upon meeting God. When we encounter beauty, goodness, and truth, we encounter God. Beauty, goodness, and truth not only guide us to this encounter but also help transform us by this encounter. Because they are qualities shared by all beings, they also shape us in a way to better encounter God and those around us. Beauty, goodness, and truth offer a deep curriculum for catechesis, one that undergirds the particular topics with a basic movement toward God.

LESSONS FROM NARCISSUS

Beauty as a transcendental quality always points beyond itself to the More. The ancient myth of Narcissus holds a valuable lesson here. Narcissus was a handsome youth who harshly rejected the affections of Echo, a nymph who was in love with him. For his harshness, he incurred punishment. One day, Narcissus saw his own image in a pool of water. He thought he was beholding a beautiful creature living in the water. He was so captivated by the beauty of the image that he fell in love with it. He remained stuck in place, unable to leave the image until he died. His story is a cautionary tale about what beauty and love are not.

Although a handsome fellow, what Narcissus saw in his own reflection was in fact not authentic beauty. Rather, it was something like a pleasing aesthetic, something enjoyable to look at. What is the difference? Authentic beauty pulls us out of ourselves and calls us beyond itself to the more, the *magis*. It is never an end in itself but a portal to discover more. Beauty is evocative; it invites us to deeper meaning. Without this invitation to transcendence, the image in the pool was just a pretty reflection.

Could the image of Narcissus in the water have become

beautiful? Yes! The image would have yielded an experience of true beauty if Narcissus would have regarded it as an entry into contemplation, an entry into deeper meaning. Instead, he saw the image as an end in itself, symbolized by the fact that he was unable to move from the spot. In truth, the image in the water became an *idol* rather than an *icon* to deeper meaning. This led to his death rather than to a deeper and more abundant life. Gazing at his own image in this way also lacked in goodness and in truth. Goodness lacked in the way the image held Narcissus captive, and truth lacked in the simple fact that Narcissus did not even recognize the image for what it was: his own reflection.

The myth also tells us that Narcissus fell in love with the image. Like beauty, love also does not fit the description of experience. Instead of loving the image, he became infatuated, even obsessed with it. As we said in Chapter 3, the meaning of love is found in God, and it constitutes the reality of our faith. To love means to move out of oneself, to offer an act of self-revelation and self-gift to another. Love calls us to transcendence: it calls us out of ourselves toward another with the whole of our being. Narcissus' obsession was far from this. He was never called out of himself, but instead was held captive in obsessing over his own reflection. Though he thought perhaps it was another creature, his confusion itself showed his lack of self-awareness and lack of sensitivity to truly relate and extend himself to another. The full context of his story affirms this: before he becomes infatuated with the image in the pool, he rejects Echo, who pines for him and repeats his words. It is Echo's unrequited love that leads Narcissus to experience his own downfall by the pool.

What can the myth of Narcissus teach evangelization and catechesis? When it comes to encountering authentic beauty, it is always an experience that calls us toward transcendence.

In being moved out of ourselves, we are moved toward God. We experience goodness and truth, and we respond in faith. Faith grows into love as we respond ever more fully, a gift of self in return to God. Narcissus teaches us that true beauty is a portal to all of this, whereas hollow aesthetic pleasure simply reflects ourselves back to us. In evangelization and catechesis, beauty is an indispensable quality to the content and method of our communication of the faith.

EVEN IN THE MIDST OF DIFFICULTIES
Pope Francis tells us that beauty is *"capable of filling life with new splendor and profound joy, even in the midst of difficulties."* In fact, the presence of beauty that is discovered in the midst of the worst tragedies always gives us pause. In the wake of a tornado, fire, or earthquake, the Blessed Mother statue of the local church stands whole and unharmed in the rubble. In the wake of terror and destruction, steel beams form a cross and stand tall above the ruins of the World Trade Center. Out of a troubled life experience comes the most vivid, compelling artwork of Vincent Van Gogh, the music of Wolfgang Amadeus Mozart, the poetry of Emily Dickinson. In the wake of the most devastating day, the sun rises again, and creation continues to live in its full *viriditas*. Recognizing beauty in these most difficult moments is to know that God is there, present in the worst of it, refusing to abandon his people. Beauty is the persistence of faith, insisting on transcendence even in the worst moments.

Beauty as expressed through art is sometimes the best way we can find meaning through the tragedies of life. Anne Frank's diary, replete with beautiful, thoughtful phrases, is evidence of the human spirit transcending the horrors of persecution during World War II. It breaks our hearts, but it gives us hope. Similarly, artwork recovered from concentration camps, such as wood carvings or pencil sketches, has a humble beauty, telling us that despite the horrific, dehumanizing context, the human spirit could not be eradicated from these prisoners. This too breaks our hearts but gives us hope. The stories and music of slaves in the American South likewise reveal the persistence of the human spirit in the dehumanizing context of slavery. Art is able to give us a language to express these complex experiences in a way that no other expression can. Through art we are able to rouse and manifest our spirit and claim its transcendence toward God. This is especially powerful in the midst of suffering, captivity, loss, tragedy, or some other difficult circumstance.

In the context of evangelization and catechesis, this transcendent role of art becomes especially important. All of us carry baggage. In one way or another, all of us feel the captivity of sin and suffering, burdens weighing us down as we walk through life. In essence the Good News speaks directly to this reality and calls us instead to freedom in Christ, whose yoke is easy and whose burden is light (Matthew 11:30). The Good News calls us to freedom and life, and art gives us a way to express our reality in a way that also reaches beyond it. In this sense, art and faith go hand in hand. Both of these call us to go deeper and beyond our present reality.

CATECHESIS CONNECTION

Inviting art and creativity into the work of catechesis inevitably brings to mind felt boards and coloring pages for children. While programs like the Catechesis of the Good Shepherd are testaments to the potential of such creative approaches, some have a difficult time picturing how this would work with adults. Would the inclusion of the arts make people uncomfortable? Would it "dumb down" the instruction? Would catechesis be reduced to sitting in a circle, doing arts and crafts, and sharing our feelings? What about actually learning the content of faith? These are fair questions founded on some legitimate concerns.

Because of the transcendent potential of both art and beauty, these concerns ought not force us to dismiss the arts altogether, especially from adult faith formation. Hands-on creativity, so effective with children, is only one way to engage the arts and to experience beauty. Many (but not all!) adults feel awkward or uncomfortable about doing a creative activity, although the present popularity of adult coloring books and "corks and canvas" parties do challenge this perception. Acknowledging this discomfort, perhaps a more accessible way to introduce the arts into catechetical instruction is by way of content. There is, of course, the beauty of nature, inspiring many of our great saints to contemplate the presence of God. There are also countless great works of visual art, music, poetry, literature, film, theater, or photography that could generate profound conversations around the content of faith or invite deeper meaning. Discovering the beauty and symbolic meaning of church architecture and furnishings (baptismal font, altar, stained glass, other artwork) presents readily available artwork for any parish. Prayerful activities like *visio divina* or Ignatian imaginative contemplation are just two ways art and imagination can inspire and enrich the spirit.

✸ *Questions for Contemplation*

- Do you have a favorite film/book/painting/composition or performance of music? What deeper meaning does this work hold for you? How does this work invite you out of yourself and toward God?

- How does beauty relate to your experience of faith? When has beauty stopped you in your tracks? What did it reveal?

- What is your experience of using the arts in catechesis? What is one thing you might try differently in light of reading this chapter?

✸ *Prayer*

Almighty God ,
You are perfect Beauty, Goodness, and Truth,
and finding these in our lives is finding icons
to contemplate your divine Mystery.
True beauty moves us to open our eyes
and to see with the eyes of faith the wonder
   of your presence in the world.
Inspire us to catechize beautifully.
We ask this in the name of your Son Jesus Christ,
by the power of the Holy Spirit.
Amen.

EPILOGUE: AVE

The papal documents used in this book have an important thing is common. They all conclude by honoring Mary, the Mother of Jesus, in a special way. She is "the star of evangelization" (EN 82), "mother and model disciple" (CT 73), "Queen of the Apostles and shining star" (John Paul I, Urbi et Orbi), "Mother of the Word and Mother of Joy" (VD 124) and "star of the new evangelization and Mother of the living Gospel" (EG 288). Mother Mary has a constant and indispensable presence surrounding our ministries of the word.

Pope Francis' words about her are especially inspiring:

> *Mary, Virgin and Mother*
> *you who moved by the Holy Spirit*
> *welcomed the word of life*
> *in the depths of your humble faith:*
> *as you gave yourself completely to the Eternal One,*
> *help us to say our own "yes"*
> *to the urgent call, as pressing as ever,*
> *to proclaim the good news of Jesus.*
> **(EG 288)**

Mary, Mother of the Word, the Mother of Evangelization and of Catechesis, pray for us!